Global Footprints in Higher Education:

Cross-Cultural Experiences of Students and Faculty at
Morgan State University

Global Footprints in Higher Education

Cross Cultural Experiences of Students and Faculty at Morgan State University

This book provides narrative cross-cultural stories written by undergraduate students, graduate students, staff, and faculty. They cover a variety experiential learning—from formal program awards to informal encounters, to travel to attend conferences, to volunteerism. Cross-cultural experiences are recognized as engines leading to global awareness. When students venture outside of their routines, their worlds become larger. This then leads to greater tolerance, more awareness, or even more possibilities in life. The students, faculty, and staff of Morgan State University (MSU) are well travelled and embrace a global perspective. Their contributions to this volume demonstrate a keen consciousness shaped by interaction with people and places outside their immediate environs. Founded in 1867, MSU provides instruction to a multiethnic, multiracial, and multinational student body. It offers more than 140 programs leading to degrees on bachelor's, master's, and doctoral levels. Its Department of World Languages & International Studies responds to national and international needs by positing language as the key to mutual understanding among nations. The Division of International Affairs supports MSU President David Wilson's commitment to the international leadership, service, and education of students, faculty, and alumni. MSU's engagement with Africa and Asia is a top priority. Eighty percent of its international students hail from Nigeria, Saudi Arabia, and Kuwait. A recurring theme in the essays is the idea that growth comes when one ventures outside of her comfort zone. One of our international students calls it "stepping out." There is much more in this volume that will intrigue, entertain, and enlighten you. More than this, reading the narratives is one of the ways readers can step out and grow.

Editors

Krishna Bista, EdD, is Professor of Higher Education in the Department of Advanced Studies, Leadership and Policy at Morgan State University, USA.

Adele Newson-Horst, PhD, is Professor of English in the Department of English and Language Arts at Morgan State University, USA.

Praise for the Book

Global Footprints in Higher Education: Cross-Cultural Experiences of Students and Faculty at Morgan State University is valuable resource for students, faculty, and researchers considering the development of intercultural competence and global mindedness in today's increasingly interconnected world.

Mei Tian, PhD
Professor, School of International Studies
Xi'an Jiaotong University, China

***

Through rich and engaging stories, this book offers important personal accounts of the challenges and triumphs of international students navigating diverse and foreign academic and cultural landscapes. This inspiring and thought-provoking collection adds to other noble qualitative documentation of the international student experience.

Anthony L. Pinder
Associate Vice President for Academic Affairs –
Internationalization & Global Engagement
Emerson College, USA

***

Without reservation, I applaud this beautiful book. Through the engaging stories, readers can follow the footprints of the students and faculty members around the world and discover the beauty that cross-cultural experiences bestow upon us.

Roger W. Anderson
Assistant Professor of International Languages & Cultures
Central State University, USA

***

The group of writers is diverse, all with a different story, shared in a unique way. The positive and negative aspects of study abroad are made clear. The personal recollections will resonate with readers regardless of previous overseas travel experience. The reflections confirm- although a privilege, study abroad/international travel is not just for the privileged.

Andrea Shelton
Professor, Health Administration
Texas Southern University, USA

***

As a global citizen, it is refreshing to being able to learn about the authors' unique global adventure and experience, as well as the teachable moments for them.

Tony Lee, PhD
Assistant Department Head & Assistant Professor
Texas A&M University-Commerce, USA

This volume collects a series of novel narrative essays that illustrate vivid cross-cultural study and research experiences shared by students and faculty at Morgan State University. These stories would help international audiences to gain insights into the cross-cultural experiences of students and faculty in and outside the United States from a comparative perspective.

Kun Dai, PhD
Assistant Professor of English
The Chinese University of Hong Kong

***

Global Footprints in Higher Education: Cross-Cultural Experiences of Students and Faculty at Morgan State University is a brilliantly curated collection of essays and narratives focusing on the cross-cultural experiences of students, faculty, and staff from Morgan State University. This book is a quintessential resource for scholars seeking to truly understand the lived experiences of the dedicated individuals who directly engage in study abroad, international studies, and global research.

Michael Kung, EdD
Director of Global Education and
Program Director for the Sustainable Design
University of Florida, USA

***

An old proverb says that one learns more by traveling ten thousand miles than reading ten thousand books. This volume shows how the footprints across the world could transform our global perspectives in higher education and far beyond, which would in time facilitate our respect to the diversity of cultures and the shared future of the world.

Yibo Yang
Associate Professor, School of International Studies
Harbin Institute of Technology, China

***

This book provides narrative cross-cultural stories written by undergraduate students, graduate students, staff, and faculty. They cover a variety of experiential learning—from formal program awards to informal encounters, to travel to attend conferences, to volunteerism. Cross-cultural experiences are recognized as engines leading to global awareness. When students venture outside of their routines, their worlds become larger. This then leads to greater tolerance, more awareness, or even more possibilities in life. The students, faculty, and staff of Morgan State University are well-traveled and embrace a global perspective.

Samson Chama
Professor & Interim Chair
Department of Social Work, Psychology and Counseling
Alabama A & M University, USA

This book is a unique compendium of study abroad and cross-cultural experiences from students, faculty, and staff. The amazing stories are entertaining, highly informative, and a great research and pedagogic resource for global learning.

Nneka Nora Osakwe, PhD
Professor of English & Provost Special Assistant of
Internationalization & Global Engagement
Albany State University, USA

***

Crossing cultural boundaries has a powerful way of shaking up one's identity and creating everlasting memories. *Global Footprints in Higher Education* presents narratives with a wide array of perspectives. While unique to each author, they are tightly connected because of the exciting momentum innate in experiencing the unfamiliar. This book is essential for anyone who is interested in studying abroad and learning about new cultures, people, languages, and locations.

Maya Fenty, PhD
Assistant Director of Student Advancement, Student Success
Case Western Reserve University, USA

***

In the globalized world, preparing today's students to take their place as global citizens with a global perception and insight is indispensable and requires faculty members and staff actively engage in the initiative. In this volume, the students, faculty, and staff of Morgan State University have demonstrated their enthusiasm, endeavors, and contributions to promoting interaction with a broader community and cultivating a cross-cultural awareness.

Lin Ge, PhD
Research Coordinator, Faculty of Social Policy Research Center
University of Regina, Canada

***

This book is a brilliant showcase of Morgan State University's students and faculty engagement activities in campus internationalization. The authentic global footprints stories of students and faculty are so inspiring and powerful to international educators who work at minority serving institutions and beyond.

Ling G. LeBeau, PhD
Associate Director of International Student Success
Syracuse University, New York, USA

Particularly for public HBCU's, this volume shows the profundity of learning that is possible through internationalizing and intercultural initiatives. Its narratives of transformational growth should light a fire at HBCUs, inviting all to bask in its warm glow.

Xin (Skye) Zhao, PhD
University Teacher/Senior Fellow of HEA
The University of Sheffield Information School, UK

***

Insightful and colorful narrations of cross-cultural lived experiences of students and faculty members. A must to read volume for future students and faculty members aspiring to experience a cross-cultural journey.

Jasvir Kaur, PhD
Senior Lecturer
LaTrobe University, Australia

***

The powerful cross-cultural essays broadened my horizon, with their insightful stories of courage, hope, compassion, support and human connections, loneliness, sadness and happiness, about embracing differences and also understanding that «people are people" despite differences, mastery, empowerment and personally growth.

Sigrid Gjøtterud
Professor, Fakultet for realfag og teknologi
Norwegian University of Life Sciences, Norway

***

No research paper will delve as deeply into the human side of interculturality as this collection of touching stories. A window to observe feelings and emotions that emphasize the power of people beyond frontiers. A beacon of empathy and solidarity that flashes how close we are.

Elena de Prada Creo
Vice Dean for International Affairs
Facultad de CC. Empresariales y Turismo, Spain

***

The book is a collection of fascinating cross-border stories which unveil the ways in which the lived experiences of international students, faculty and staff are powerfully transformed through cross-cultural experiences, interactions and relationships with known and unknown worlds.

Leonardo Veliz
Senior Lecturer in Teaching, Learning and Inclusive Education
University of New England, Australia

Academic Book Series

Call for Book Proposals

The STAR Scholars Book Series seeks to explore new ideas and best practices related to international student mobility, study abroad, exchange programs, student affairs from the US and around the world, and from a wide range of academic fields, including student affairs, international education, and cultural studies. STAR Scholars publishes some titles in collaboration with Routledge (Taylor & Francis), Springer, Palgrave Macmillan, Open Journals in Education (OJED), Journal of International Students, and other university presses. Scholars interested in contributing a book to our current and future book series are invited to submit a brief proposal directly via this form. All chapters will go through the standard review process before a decision is made.
https://www.ojed.org/index.php/gsm/Series

Series Editors

Dr. Chris R. Glass & Dr. Krishna Bista

For questions and submission, email at Krishna.bista@morgan.edu

Recently Published Books

1. *Chinese Students and the Experience of International Doctoral Study in STEM*
2. *Developing Intercultural Competence in Higher Education*
3. *International Student Mobility to and from the Middle East*
4. *Inequalities in Study Abroad and Student Mobility*
5. *The Experiences of International Faculty in Institutions of Higher Education*
6. *International Students at US Community Colleges*
7. *Critical Perspectives on Equity and Social Mobility in Study Abroad*
8. *Online Teaching, Learning and Virtual Experiences in Global Higher Education*
9. *International Student Support and Engagement in Higher Education*
10. *Impact of COVID-19 on Global Student Mobility and Higher Education*
11. *Global Higher Education During COVID-19: Policy, Society, and Technology*
12. *COVID-19 and Higher Education in the Global Context*
13. *Reimagining Mobility in Higher Education*
14. *Cross-Cultural Narratives: Stories and Experiences of International Students*
15. *Reimagining Internationalization and International Initiatives at HBCUs*
16. *Delinking, Relinking, and Linking Writing and Rhetorics*

Open Journals in Education (OJED) at STAR Scholars publishes high quality peer reviewed, open access journals based at research universities. OJED uses the Open Journal System platform, where readers can browse by subject, drill down to journal level to find the aims, scope, and editorial board for each individual title, as well as search back issues. None of the OJED journals charge fees to individual authors thanks to the generous support of our institutional sponsors. OJED journals benefit from the editorial, production, and marketing expertise of our team of volunteers.

Explore our journals at www.ojed.org

Higher Education Politics & Economics

Journal of Comparative and International Higher Education

Journal of Underrepresented & Minority Progress

Journal of Human Services

Journal of Interdisciplinary Studies in Education

Journal of Development Education

Journal of Trauma Studies in Education

Journal of School Administration Research and Development

Journal of Global Literacies, Technologies & Emerging Pedagogies

International Journal of Multidisciplinary Perspectives in Higher Education

Global Footprints in Higher Education

Stories and Experiences of International Students

Edited by

Krishna Bista
Department of Advanced Studies, Leadership and Policy
Morgan State University, USA

Adele Newson-Horst
Department of English
Morgan State University, USA

First Published 2022

by

STAR Scholars

In collaboration with

Open Journals in Education

Journal of International Students

Category

Education/International Students

Series

Comparative and International Education

Editors
Krishna Bista
Adele Newson-Horst

ISBN: 978-1-957480-01-5

© STAR Scholars

Library of Congress Control Number:
2022936497

Global Footprints in Higher Education:
Cross Cultural Experiences of Students and
Faculty at Morgan State University

Subject: Education/International Students –
United States | International Education |
Student Mobility | Comparative Education

Names: Krishna Bista (editor), Adele
Newson-Horst (series editor)

Library of Congress
US Programs, Law, and Literature Division
Cataloging in Publication Program
101 Independence Avenue, S.E.
Washington, DC 20540-4283

Typeset in Garamond

Project Judges
Abigail Higgs
Russel Davis

Cover Design
Costanza Lettieri

Printed in the United States of America

On cover image illustration, two figures are divided by a border but connected through a book-- a symbol of culture, exchange, and freedom.

Facts and opinions published in this book express solely the opinions of the respective authors. Authors are responsible for their citing of sources and the accuracy of their references and bibliographies. The editor, series editor or the publisher cannot be held responsible for any lacks or possible violations of third parties' rights.

Contents

Foreword - M'bare N'gom   xv
Acknowledgement   xvi
Introduction   xvii

PART I
Study Abroad Experiences of American Students

1. The Cuban Revolution: Unlocking the Power of Literacy   3
   David Miller, United States
2. The Wonders of Cape Town   7
   Rachael Falu, United States
3. My Adventure to Spain Started in New Jersey   10
   Ry'yana King, United States
4. Visual Art in Motion: Analyzing Strength, Culture, and History Abroad   15
   Dara Sennaar, United States
5. A Transformational Journey   19
   Katrina L. Pitts, United States
6. I Reached My Goal of a PhD through International Study   23
   R. Jerome Anderson, United States
7. The Semester of My Dreams in Madrid, Spain   26
   Janice Alonzo, United States
8. A Tale of a New City   30
   Sierra DeLoatch, United States
9. Unique Experiences Through Study Abroad   34
   Samala B. Lewis, United States
10. Ghana as the Gateway to International Travel   36
    Fawaz Abdullah, United States
11. Travel through Association   38
    Keivon Anderson, United States
12. Similarities are Greater than Differences   39
    Dale Plater, The Bahamas
13. Internationally Non-Traditional   41
    Dominique Turner, United States
14. In the Kingdom   44
    Jameeka Michelle Gillis, United States
15. Culture Shock in my Culture   47
    Jennifer Dasilva-Hassiman, Venezuela

PART II
Experiences of International Students in the United States

16. My International Experience in the United States   53
    Abisola Arowolaju, Nigeria
17. When I Grow Up, I Want to Be an Oreo   56
    Ife Adedoyin, Nigeria
18. American Hunger   58
    Ruth Amara Okolo, Nigeria
19. International Student Experience: Land of the Free   60
    Omolade Ola, Nigeria
20. My Experience as an International Student during the COVID 63
    Pandemic
    Tolulope Ajayi, Nigeria
21. My Cross-Cultural Study Experience: An American Dream   65
    Achieved
    Fatima K. Babih, Sierra Leone
22. Postgraduate Studies: A Lifelong Experience on Teaching and 68
    Learning
    Shuaibu Hassan Usman, Nigeria
23. Long Way to the United States   71
    Ramina Javid, Iran
24. Fortitude and Perseverance in the Face of Discomforts,   73
    Discouragements, and Challenges
    Antonia Nwogbo, Nigeria
25. Colour, Color, Me   77
    Martha Kakooza, Uganda
26. From Kenya to the US: My Experience of Completing a   80
    Master's Degree at an HBCU
    Collins Oswago, Kenya
27. Becoming a Morganite   84
    Abubakar S. Ringim, Nigeria
28. A New Culture: A New Style of Learning   89
    Freda Alabi, Nigeria
29. My Experience as an International Student in America   93
    Otily Toutsop, Cameroon
30. Amelican Palava: Words, World, or Wonder   96
    Jennifer Umezinwa, Nigeria
31. Resilience! My Watchword in My New Home   99
    Bukola Daramola, Nigeria

PART III
Cross Cultural Experiences of Faculty and Staff

32. The Fulbright Narrative: The South African Experience   105
     Adele Newson-Horst, United States
33. The Organizational Ombudsman and the Cross-Cultural   114
     Experience
     Wilbur Hicks, United States
34. I Am not Your Black Diamond: Breaking the Silence after   117
     Eleven Years
     Sharlene Allen-Milton, United States
35. Learning Language, Learning Philosophy   122
     Seth Vannatta, United States
36. Intellectual and Cultural Humility: My reflection on a Series of 124
     Moments during the Ghana Excursion
     Dia Sekayi, United States
37. Learning Beyond the Curriculum   128
     Gonzalo Baptista, United States
38. A Divine Encounter to Remember   133
     Jacqueline Holland, United States
39. Diversifying the Colonized Mind in the Warmth of an HBCU   136
     Denise Jarrett, United States
40. Not in My Classroom   140
     Kimberly McManus, United States
41. Better Together: Team Teaching Across Cultures in the Age of   143
     Uncertainty
     E. Blaise DePaolo, United States
     Susan J. Langford, United Kingdom
42. Kabwalala! The Bantu Word that Saved & Changed My Life   148
     Anita Pandey, United States

     Epilogue   159
     Further Readings   160
     About the Editors   162

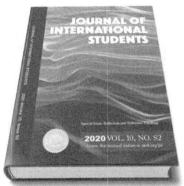

To order online, visit
www.ojed.org/jis

Paperback and e-books
available.

Foreword

Global Footprints in Higher Education: Cross-Cultural Experiences of Students and Faculty at Morgan State University explores and reflects on the ways engagement with international communities through a wide range of meaningful academic and project-based activities significantly improves education. The book offers diverse perspectives on transnational experiential learning, teaching, research, service, and internship as an academic and skills building value-added proposition geared to achieve and enhance linguistic, cultural, and communicative proficiency. Overall, the different essays contend that, "The learning process includes the transition from a local view (local used here as a synonym of national culture) to a cosmopolitan view and understanding of the world" (Goncalves, 2010). Global engagement, in my opinion, and as argued in different chapters of the book, aims to foster diversity and cross-cultural understanding by placing stakeholders, students, faculty, and staff, in intentional situations where they are immersed in multiple transactions and learning opportunities that will enable them to communicate with people from diverse backgrounds, partner, collaborate, and eventually, become globally competent professionals and compassionate citizens. Additionally, the book proposes tangible strategies on the implementation of meaningful and high impact transnational experiential learning, study, research, service, and internship activities that aim "to increase global competencies" and the acquisition of "21st century skills applied to the world," consistent with Morgan State University efforts to expand its global footprint. This book will be a valuable resource to those who are interested in global education, for it provides unique experiences about the limitless possibilities of cross-border and transnational education.

References

Goncalves, S. (2010). The imperative for international education. *Exedra, Revista Científica*, 1, 13-28.

M'BARE N'GOM, PhD, is Professor and Dean in the James H. Gilliam, Jr. College of Liberal Arts at Morgan State University, Maryland, USA.

Acknowledgements

We are truly grateful to all the Morgan State University students who participated in this "Morgan Global Footprints" project beginning the fall of 2021, and to the staff and faculty who encouraged them to write and share their stories. We are also grateful to the faculty and staff who contributed their narratives to this work.

We would like to express our sincere thanks Dr. David Kwabena Wilson, President, Morgan State University for his support of and vision of our global research institution. Also, thanks to the Division of Academic Affairs and the Division of International Affairs for their leadership and support. Special thanks go to all the judges who have volunteered to read the essays and offer their feedback: Prof. Abagail Higgs and Dr. Russell Davis.

We express my appreciation to Dr. Uttam Gaulee (STAR Scholars, President), Dr. Chris Glass (STAR Scholars, VP), and colleagues at the STAR Scholars Network and at the Open Journals in Education, a consortium of the professional journals, for their assistance and coordination in publishing this book. Without their support and guidance, this book would not have become a reality.

We would like to thank the following colleagues for their feedback on the early draft of this book as well as for their endorsements:

- *Andrea Shelton, Texas Southern University, USA*
- *Anthony L. Pinder, Emerson College, USA*
- *Jasvir Kaur, LaTrobe University, Australia*
- *Kun Dai, The Chinese University of Hong Kong*
- *Lin Ge, University of Regina, Canada*
- *Ling G. LeBeau, Syracuse University, New York, USA*
- *Maya Fenty, Case Western Reserve University, USA*
- *Mei Tian, Xi'an Jiaotong University, China*
- *Michael Kung, University of Florida, USA*
- *Nneka Nora Osakwe, Albany State University, USA*
- *Roger W. Anderson, Central State University, USA*
- *Samson Chama, Alabama A&M University, USA*
- *Tony Lee, Texas A&M University-Commerce, USA*
- *Xin (Skye) Zhao, The University of Sheffield, UK*
- *Yibo Yang, Harbin Institute of Technology, China*

Krishna Bista
Adele Newson-Horst

Introduction

Cross-cultural experiences are recognized as engines leading to global awareness. When students venture outside of their routines, their worlds become larger. This then leads to greater tolerance, more awareness, or even more possibilities in life. The students, faculty, and staff at Morgan State University (MSU)—are well travelled and embrace a global perspective. Their contributions to this volume demonstrate a keen consciousness shaped by interaction with people and places outside their immediate environs.

Founded in 1867, MSU provides instruction to a multiethnic, multiracial, and multinational student body. It offers more than 140 programs leading to degrees on the BA/BS, master's, and PhD levels. Its Department of World Languages & International Studies responds to national and international needs by positing language as the key to mutual understanding among nations. The Division of International Affairs supports MSU President David Wilson's commitment to the international leadership, service, and education of students, faculty, and alumni. The two entities along with other academic units are committed to producing and supporting a campus of global citizens equipped for competition in an interdependent society and economy.

MSU's engagement with Africa and Asia is a top priority. Eighty percent of its international students hail from Nigeria, Saudi Arabia, and Kuwait. Additionally, the institution has a record breaking 12 memos of understanding with Nigerian institutions, alone! Additionally, the Division of International Affairs is actively seeking to grow its relationships with East and Sub-Saharan Africa, China, and Southeast Asian nations throughout 2018-2024. With the support of the entire Morgan family, Assistant Vice President for International Affairs Dr. Yacob Astatke explains that "we look forward to building exciting new partnerships and cross-cultural programming to continue growing the future, leading the world." Relatedly, MSU leads all other historically Black colleges and universities in the number of its students who have participated in the Fulbright program having received 140 Fulbright or Fulbright-related grants in 44 countries.

There are 42 essays contained in this volume written by undergraduate students, graduate students, staff, and faculty. They cover a variety of experiential learning—from formal program awards to informal encounters, to travel to attend conferences, to volunteerism. One student endured 15 hours of travel amid the COVID pandemic to enroll in MSU's engineering program. Yet another student experienced art in a foreign land that provides a corrective to historical records. Comparing MSU's educational system to his home country's approach to teaching, a student found that he had to adjust his learning style from a passive one to an active one where he discovered that his MSU professors actually had an interest in his ideas. Another entry makes the discovery that "You cannot believe everything you read and hear about other places, but you must experience them yourself." One of the professors discovers a fundamental truth about nationalities based on how countries teach their students to read. Yet another student advised that the best international travel is best achieved by a consideration of input from students.

All the essays in this book offer a rich descriptive account of the authors' personal journey of studying or working in another place or country. Their stories and encounters with people who speak or look differently, their academic or cultural integration with people who act differently, and their perseverance and sacrifice to enrich their lives make this book meaningful. Where did international students come from at Morgan State University? Where did African American students go to study abroad? And what do faculty and staff cross-cultural experiences look like at Morgan State University? This book is a testimony of why these brave scholars choose to travel, study, or live abroad and become global citizens developing a comprehensive understanding of people, places, languages, and cultures other than their own.

It is particularly important for minority students and faculty to expand their understanding of the world and to challenge the stereotypes and myths or deficit narratives about the Black experience in America and abroad.

Many students who elect to study in the US seek a better education and remind us of their struggles against social discrimination and injustices, poverty and hunger, and violence and crime. Their narratives contribute to the transformation of mindsets of the American people and beyond. Likewise, many American students travel abroad to study and broaden their mindset and garner a respect for our larger global society. Despite the COVID-19 global pandemic, the war in Ukraine, the discourse of geopolitical tensions, and natural disasters, we seek peace, knowledge, harmony, and understanding of each other.

This book is a piece of the larger puzzle that documents cross-cultural narratives of minorities students at historically Black colleges and universities (HBCUs) and beyond. In the United States, there are 104 HBCUs (53 public and 51 private nonprofit institutions) located in 19 states and the U.S. Virgin Islands. About 12,000 international students pursue degrees in various disciplines and programs at HBCUs and most of them come from Sub-Saharan Africa, Latin America and the Caribbean, the Middle East, North Africa, Europe, and Asia. The top ten places of origin for international students at HBCUs include Nigeria, Saudi Arabia, Jamaica, Bahamas, India, Dominica, Kuwait, Nepal, Kenya, and Ghana. On the other hand, a small percentage of African American students (0.7%) at HBCUs go abroad out of 347,099 total enrollments. The top destinations for HBCU students traveling abroad include Spain, China, the United Kingdom, Italy, Singapore, Mexico, Jamaica, Costa Rica, Colombia, and the Dominican Republic.

We are proud to present the winning names for the student essays in the Morgan Global Footprints Competition:

Graduate Student Category:
First Place - David C. Miller, International Exchange Experience
Second Place - Rachael Falu, Study Abroad Experience
Third Place - Ruth Okola, International Student Experience
Honorable Mention- Jennifer Umezinwa, International Student Experience

Undergraduate Student Category:
First Place - Ifeoluwa Adedoyin, International Exchange Experience
Second Place - Dara Sennaar, Study Abroad Experience
Third Place - Ryyana King, Study Abroad Experience
Honorable Mention - Abisola Arowolaju, International Student Experience

A recurring theme in the essays is the idea that growth comes when one ventures outside of her comfort zone. One of our international students calls it "stepping out." There is much more in this volume that will intrigue, entertain, and enlighten you. More than this, reading the narratives is one of the ways readers can step out and grow.

KRISHNA BISTA is a Professor of Higher Education in the Department of Advanced Studies, Leadership and Policy at Morgan State University, Maryland (USA).

ADELE NEWSON-HORST is a Professor of English in the Department of English and Language Arts at Morgan State University, Maryland (USA).

PART I

Study Abroad Experiences of American Students

1

The Cuban Revolution: Unlocking the Power of Literacy

David Miller, *United States*

While growing up on the west side of Baltimore, my life was filled with a host of unanticipated obstacles and challenges. My parents, Peter and Carol Miller, realized their best chance at educating and socializing two, energetic Black male children was immersing them in books. My mom, a high school home economics teacher, enforced weekly reading and prepared reading comprehension assignments to supplement our public-school education.

My indoctrination into books began early in my academic career with weekly trips to the Enoch Pratt Free Library and a subscription to *National Geographic* magazine. Every month, I anxiously awaited my new edition of the magazine and would rush home from school to check the mailbox. As an impressionable young reader, the magazine introduced me to breathtaking photos of life in Africa, Asia, Latin America, and Europe that adorned its pages. Many of my earliest geography lessons came from stories I read in the magazine about exotic foods, tribal customs, and spiritual practices.

While most of my peers in Baltimore dreamed of life as professional athletes, I yearned for a career that enabled me to jump on planes and travel overseas. Armed with a passport and stories from the magazines, my goal was to become a global citizen who traveled internationally to work on and champion human rights.

Numerous times over the last decade I've traveled to Ghana in West Africa to support literacy work and donate children's books written by Black American authors to rural villages. The entire time, I also longed to visit Havana, Cuba.

Historically, the struggles of Cuba and Anti-American sentiment levied against Fidel Castro have been fascinating. I've read everything I could get my hands on about Castro, Che Guevara, Antonio Maceo, José Martí, other lesser-known freedom fighters and the Cuban Revolution. Like many Black Americans, I was mesmerized by Assata Shakur's narrative, her relocation to Cuba and many other untold stories seldom recognized in the U.S.

I was intrigued by the student-led protests, during the early stages of the Cuban Revolution, poverty, unemployment, and the stark difference between literacy rates in urban communities and rural sections of Cuba. These student protests were similar to the student-led protests in the U.S. during the modern civil rights movement.

In January 2019, my dreams came true when I traveled to Havana, Cuba, as part of a Black Writers and Publishers delegation for the Feria Internacional del Libro de La Habana (28th Havana International Book Fair). The book festival honored the literacy work seeded during the Cuban Revolution and attracted over half a million visitors.

The delegation featured several of the oldest and most prominent Black publishers in the U.S., including Third World Press - Haki R. Madhubuti (Founded in 1967), Black Classic Press - W. Paul Coates (Founded in 1978), Just Us Books - Wade and Cheryl Willis Hudson (Founded in 1988), and a host of other writers, bibliophiles and literacy activists.

Our delegation toured several cultural and educational places representing significant landmarks essential to Cuba's rich history. We visited the Museo Nacional de la Alfabetización (National Museum of the Literacy Campaign), reviewing exhibits featuring film footage, photos and personal documents of volunteers involved in Cuba's historic literacy campaign. The museum chronicled Conrado Benitez Brigadistas, mobilizing two hundred fifty-thousand volunteers to travel to remote sections of Cuba to teach children reading and writing. By 1961, with an audacious literacy strategy, Cuba became one of the most literate countries in the world, according to The United Nations Educational, Scientific and Cultural Organization (UNESCO).

Additionally, we visited Biblioteca Nacional José Martí (The José Martí National Library), a unique national treasure featuring over four million titles. Founded in 1901, the national library is a magnificent structure with critical cultural artifacts, books and documents honoring Cuba and its influences on Latin America.

During this historic visit, our delegation presented officials from The José Martí National Library with a collection of books written by us to be housed as part of the library's standing collection. These books included historical fiction, poetry, and children's books.

We also visited Matanzas, the second largest province in Cuba and the home of the largest population of Afro-Cubans. Matanzas is also known for practitioners of the Santería and cultural influences, including the Yoruba religion. In the 1850s it was estimated that seventy percent of Matanzas were enslaved people forced to work the sugar plantations, which created economic wealth for Cuba. While visiting Matanzas, our delegation donated school supplies, money, and books to a thriving community center supporting Afro-Cubans. We were fortunate to meet and spend time with several activists intimately involved in Castro's literacy campaign as volunteers. These experiences provided our delegation with deep historical context to understand the power of the Cuban Revolution and the will of the Cuban people.

The highlight of our visit to Cuba was participating in the book festival, a government-supported event that attracted half a million people. Schools are closed during the book festival, and families attend by the thousands to support literacy. As far as the eye could see, there were long lines of families purchasing books of all genres. Suffice it to say it was heartwarming. Spending time in a country that prioritizes literacy was a humbling experience that I think about often as I wrestle with the alarming literacy challenges impacting low-income communities — with mostly Black and brown residents -- in the U.S.

During the book festival, Rosemari Mealy, the trip's organizer and author of *Fidel and Malcolm: Memories of a Meeting*, presented her new book to a robust audience of Cubans. Her book reflects on the historic encounter between Castro and Malcolm X at the Hotel Theresa in Harlem, New York, on Sept. 19, 1960. Mealy was one of three U.S. journalists invited to participate in this historic meeting between two revered yet controversial revolutionaries.

For me, the experience was surreal. Sitting on the back of a bus while riding around Havana listening to Mealy was illuminating. As was the case with many Black males, my discovery of Malcolm X's autobiography was a game-changer and listening to firsthand accounts of the meeting between Castro and Malcolm X was most memorable.

Our cultural experience included a visit to the park on Avenida 23 between Calle F and Calle E, honoring Dr. Martin Luther King, Jr. and Malcolm X. The

Cuban government commissioned a dual plaque to celebrate these Black American icons revered by Castro.

My trip to Cuba was a unique cultural experience that heightened my awareness of the complex history of Castro and the struggles of Cuba in modern times. Moreover, the trip provided me with a deeper understanding of the uniqueness of socialism and the painful experiences of many Cuban Americans.

Spending ten days in Cuba while doing literacy work and meeting many grassroots individuals involved in "literacy activism" solidified my commitment to accelerate my literacy work. Cuba has provided an important model that should be studied and replicated globally to increase efforts to address illiteracy.

On our last day in Cuba, I spent time at La Terraza de Cojímar, a frequent watering hole of iconic American writer Ernest Hemingway. Overlooking the Cojímar Bay, the restaurant served as a "cultural backdrop" for many of Hemingway's most essential novels.

People often cite the phrase, "trip of a lifetime." Well, the trip to Cuba with fellow Black writers and publishers certainly ranks among the most meaningful of my life, and I am profoundly grateful I got to experience it.

DAVID C. MILLER frequently leads intergenerational conversations with men and boys focused on fatherhood, mental health, managing anger, decision making, and navigating encounters with the police. Miller's work has appeared on CNN, NPR, PBS, MSNBC, and in the *Huffington Post* (US & Canada), *BBC Magazine, Baltimore Sun,* and a host of other media outlets. Miller has published several scholarly articles, essays, and book chapters, which appear in academic periodicals and publications. Miller is a 2022 Fulbright-Hays Study Abroad Fellow (Ghana). Miller is a Ph.D. Candidate in the School of Social Work at Morgan State University, focusing on Black fatherhood. E-mail: damil22@morgan.edu

2

The Wonders of Cape Town

Rachael Falu, *United States*

With only two students enrolled in my course, I was awed when my South African/African American Literature course was accepted into a Consortium that would allow me to travel and teach in Cape Town, South Africa for three weeks. I'd never been to Africa and was eager to travel. I assumed I'd teach my students, visit incredible places, and meet new people. Being a Black woman in America, I felt strongly that I had a firm grasp on marginalization and all the way my identity othered me. Still, I was wrong and had shortchanged my experience regarding the privileges of life had also granted me. What I underestimated most was how much I would learn from my students.

Our time in Cape Town was to be focused on scholarship and service. We went on all the traditional touristy excursions, Robben Island, where President Nelson Mandela was imprisoned for almost three decades, Table Mountain, and the townships that were rebuilding after Apartheid. Our time in the districts, museums, and evaluating the history of South Africa imprinted one thing on my mind: the United States is not alone in maintaining and perpetuating the oppression of Blacks.

At the time, there were fourteen official languages and fourteen political parties in South Africa. President Jacob Zuma was newly elected to office, mostly by citizens born post-Apartheid, called *freeborns*. There was an effervescent feeling to the Cape signaling that the times were changing. Ami, our program director, had arranged two service-learning opportunities. The first was at Ons Plek; Ons Plek is Afrikans for Our Place, and the facility served as after-school assistance for children. I immensely enjoyed every moment with those children. We played games, served lunch, and learned more about their culture. The second service opportunity did not go as planned. The supervisor at the orphanage disagreed with Ami on our allotted time and wanted money, so we no longer went back to the orphanage.

The tension from the altercation at the orphanage led to rumors being spread amongst the students, and Ami declared that we would have chats every evening after dinner. During chats, students and faculty were given the opportunity to discuss the revelations and realizations we had throughout the day. These conversations were most enlightening. Our schedule was planned out months before we departed from Tennessee, but due to fallout with the orphanage, we had extra time in our schedule. Rather than being allowed to explore Cape Town freely, Ami, who had an infatuation with the aquatic birds, took us on our third visit to see penguins. These visits were getting monotonous, and surely there was more to see in the Cape than birds. One night during a chat, a student, Jolynn, mentioned that the trip was disappointing. She asserted that she was a first-generation college student, worked throughout high school and college, acquired a scholarship to travel to Cape Town, and figured it would be years before she could travel abroad again. She felt that more attention and time had been given to birds than to Cape Town. This testimony was eye-opening and humbling for me. I was bored and only thought of my time there as work. I'd selfishly failed to see what this opportunity meant for our students. Jolynn's declaration was well received by the students, but it saddened Ami. Her intention was not to diminish their experience, but she did disregard the idea that she was blocking a wholly immersive involvement with Cape Town.

I was proud of Jolynn. She boldly advocated for the type of experience she wanted. This act humbled me. At 21, I never would have done that. I would have passively complained, but she was fearless. I now try to consider trips from all perspectives and that students' input should be included in the planning of their trips; hopefully, if they are given some authority, they will be more invested and proactive to research the area prior to travel. Unfortunately, Jolynn highlighted a familiar issue with trips to Africa. Most Black Americans feel a connection to Africa, but America's media has skewed our perception of the motherland and given an outlook of the continent that reinforces negative stereotypes. Nevertheless, this monolithic mindset had seeped into the planning of our trip and prevented us from experiencing Cape Town organically.

I am forever grateful to Jolynn for highlighting an issue with the scheduling and calling attention to the type of trip she felt she deserved versus the one she was receiving. From her and other students, I learned to always advocate for what I feel I deserve and not settle for less so others can feel validated. I no longer violate my boundaries. International travel is a privilege and one that should be regarded as such. Despite its reputation, Cape Town is a gorgeous city and rich in culture and beauty. Although Cape Town initially seemed different from Tennessee, it was not. It was a place whose legacy was tainted with racism, where a reckoning was occurring.

RACHAEL FALU is a doctoral student in the English Department. Her major research interests are Gothicism and 19th and 20th century African American Literature. Email: Rafal1@gmail.com

3

My Adventure to Spain Started in New Jersey

Ry'yana King, *United States*

When I was a sophomore at Hudson Catholic Regional High School, my school began promoting a new student exchange program. It was to a private Catholic school in McGinley Square, Jersey City, New Jersey. My school had a small population of five-hundred students, which was small compared to the local public schools. It valued diversity, so our student population consisted of all racial groups including Asian, African-American, Caucasian, Hispanic, or mixed. Hudson Catholic had endless resources and opportunities, so we were given the chance to study education abroad. The year was 2019, and we collaborated with a school in Pontevedra, Spain. I was chosen along with two other students, Sofia and Angelina, to take the chance to study abroad. I was very excited since I had never traveled outside the country. I never even took an airplane. I've been on road trips to visit my distant family that lives in the tristate area but that wasn't far away, still close to home. I was thrilled to be riding on a plane for the very first time. All I could think about was sitting in the window seat, looking at the blue skies and fluffy clouds. I had the opportunity to explore, and try new things, and I would be surrounded by a different culture other than my own.

In the student exchange program, three students from Los Sauces would study at Hudson Catholic from September to November, while residing in the homes of the students at Hudson. Sofia, Angelina and I would then study and reside in the students' homes in Los Sauces, Spain, from February to May. Jersey City is a small area with a large population. Jersey City was listed as the second most diverse city in America. The city is broken into many sections including the Downtown area, Greenville, The Heights, McGinley Square and Westside. The area I live in is the Greenville section and is mostly filled with middle-class families. There are also people who live or work in that section who are helped by government assistance or financially they can't afford to live anywhere else. Living there has been uneasy; the violence and crime rates are high;

the community isn't safe, and it is hard to move out once you've in. Since I was a kid, I had imagined seeing more than what was going on in my community, and I got that opportunity when given the chance to study abroad.

My family and I were very excited to host a student for the first time; it was something I wanted to do since I was a kid. My mom and stepmom were stunned at first. We didn't live in the best part of the community, and my mom was gay. But that didn't matter to me, I wanted to give someone the same chance I had. When I told my brothers Zaire, Kevin, and Zion that Zaira would be staying with us they all agreed, "Ho'boy another girl living in the house, what a tragedy!" They weren't as thrilled as me but I was happy. I was the oldest and only girl out of three boys. Finally, I would have the chance to connect with someone of my own age and gender. Growing up as the only girl was hard and rough and being the oldest didn't make it better.

I wanted everything to be perfect and comfortable for Zaira. I had waited a long time to meet her and my family prepared a lot for her arrival. Prior to Zaira's arrival, I redecorated my room so that we had more space and she would feel at home. I also resigned from my part-time job. I would not be able to work and spend time with Zaira. A lot of sacrifices were made so that Zaira could live with me. Although tough decisions were made I was still excited to meet her and I couldn't wait to amaze her. The neighborhood isn't the best sightseeing place but there are some wonderful places around Jersey City.

My mom and I picked Zaira up from the JFK airport in New York City. I was finally meeting her for the first time. When I saw her standing across from me, I was speechless. Her hair was dark brown and long and her skin was fuzzy like a peach. I imagined her to be tall, but she was shorter than me. She had a distinguished scent to her; it smelled like sweet roses and strawberries. Her voice was soft and she seemed to always be cheerful. Prior to that, we would communicate over Whatsapp or Instagram, but actually seeing her was a dream come true. In my head I thought, "Finally she's here, my new best friend". When I was helping her grab her luggage we both bump heads and from that I thought it was too good to be true. Just before we all got home, I showed Zaira around the community. Houses around the area were in all shapes and sizes. There were houses and apartment buildings; and stores were on every corner. She was amazed at how all the houses and stores were close together, and she had told me that in Spain everything is more spacious and farther apart. The area wasn't particularly a clean place, trash covered the streets.

11

Zaira told me that in Spain the streets are spotless; many of the homes were staggered on a mountain and that they have numerous shopping stores. She looked surprised and shocked at the same time; it was as if she didn't believe it.

Hosting Zaira at my home was only momentary, though. Within the two days that she had been staying with me and my family, I guess she didn't feel quite comfortable. Although I went to a Catholic school, and my mom was gay, I never felt any discrimination from my school. Zaira's parents were strict Catholics, and they didn't approve of their daughter's surroundings, even though she didn't care. I couldn't understand or realize what the problem was; I thought she was happy and comfortable. Her parents didn't want Zaira to live in a same gender house, and since we were sharing a room they felt even more uncomfortable. They also mentioned that our community wasn't safe enough for her. Having Zaira relocated to a new home was devastating to me because I didn't want her to leave, and neither did she. There were underlying reasons unsaid, but I was too young to understand.

Although Zaira wasn't living with me anymore, that didn't keep us from being together. Zaira was bright, amusing, and fashionable. At the time we both were listening to Korean boy band "BTS" and we both had the hots for Kim-Nam-Joon aka RM. In school we had the same schedule, so we did everything together. Lunchtime was always the best because we got to see Sofia and Angelina, and the other exchange students, Julia and Daniella. Whenever I didn't have practice or a game, I would take Zaira out to see some places around Jersey City. I was depressed not having Zaira live with me because I thought it would have been much cooler, but I didn't let that stop us from having fun. As Zaira and I spent time together, she really opened up to me, and we were like sisters, even in that short period of time. During our time together Zaira celebrated Thanksgiving, we went to Washington D.C and visited all the amusement parks in the tristate. Zaira left in November, just before Christmas. It was hard having to say goodbye because I knew that I had to finish the semester without her until February.

When I left in February, I was a bit homesick because I had never been away by myself or even away from my family. But I had my classmates Sofia and Angelina with me and that helped. While waiting for my flight, I couldn't stop thinking about all the new things that I wanted to try or see. I thought about leaving my family. The feeling was frightening but I couldn't stop thinking about Zaira. The flight was long, and our first stop was in Dublin. The airport was quiet; I guess that was because it was dark and early when we landed. We had to wait two hours before our next flight to Madrid. When we arrived in Madrid the airport was loud, and they had everything. They had all types of shopping stores, food restaurants, and more. It was like a huge shopping extravaganza and I didn't want to leave. Since Pontevedra is a small city in Spain, there was no airport.

So, from Madrid we took another flight to Vigo, which is closer to Pontevedra. Finally arriving in Pontevedra, I got to meet Zaira and her family. Meeting her family was comforting but a bit difficult. Only Zaira and her brother Hector knew English so in order for me to speak to her parents, they had to translate everything for me. After meeting Zaira's family, I headed to the school Los Sauces. I didn't expect to be living by myself, but Zaira's parents thought it was more convenient. Zaira tried to convince her parents to allow me to stay, but they argued that it would be unfitting. Sofia and Angelina had the privilege of staying with Julia and Danielle, while I was by myself. Los Sauces is a private regional school for all students that live in Spain. Kids from all over Spain would travel to go there, so it became a boarding school.

First Day in Spain/ Angelina(on the left)Sofia, me, and Tatiyana (on the right)

Living in a boarding school wasn't as bad as I thought it would be. I was lonely for a bit, also home-sick. When school started, I was nervous because I was the only brown student, and you could tell that I was American. The students at Los Sauces were all very helpful and kind. I took the similar classes as I would back at home, except they added music, a foreign language class, and we had swimming lessons. During my three months in Pontevedra, I got to venture out to see a lot of different places in the city. Around the city there were always statues, churches, fountains, street entertainers, and street merchants. I learned how to play the piano and I met a bunch of interesting people. I formed bonds with most of them. My favorite part about Spain was the food. Almost every day, I would go out to eat something new and different every time. If I had a time machine, I would go back and relive those three months again. Even though I missed being away from home, I really enjoyed my independence and my time over there. Still to this day I am in contact with the friends that I made over in Spain.

RY'YANA KING (originally from the US) is an undergraduate student in the Department of Elementary Education. Her major research interest includes creative thinking, volunteering, and leadership skills.

4

Visual Art in Motion: Analyzing Strength, Culture, and History Abroad

Dara Sennaar, *United States*

Art is powerful. In my opinion, it's one of the greatest gifts humankinds has ever been blessed with. It's omnipresent and can take on an infinite number of forms. "Art imitating life" and "Life imitating art" are the same. There is beauty, ugliness, and pain in life that has been and continues to be reflected in art. In addition, thriving in life is an art. My perspective on life has formed through creative and artistic lenses. My recent trip to Belgium gave me invaluable opportunities to take on the artistic journey of a lifetime.

In Brussels with a Historical Context

In October 2021, I was blessed to travel to Brussels with my aunt, who is an artist herself. Taking this trip, especially with her, compelled me to embrace the art around me, and be present in the beauty, as well as the ugliness I saw. Being that I live in a society that prioritizes capitalistic success, I'm not in the habit of simply being present. However, this trip helped me realize the importance of living in the moment and fully participating in the world around me. Living presently helps me to stay grounded, aware, and sane, while navigating challenging experiences. The majority of my reflection was done in Brussels, Belgium. My aunt believed it important to embrace the historical context of the country we were visiting. So, we visited the Royal Museum of Central Africa. Primarily, this museum used art and historical artifacts to rationalize the past. In particular, the history of colonization of Belgium that was once prized and celebrated by its dominant culture, was on display and explained away, rather than reconciled.

Leaving the Past Behind: Aimé Mpane's Transformative Work
However, a powerful exhibit that shattered this objective was that of Congolese artist Aimé Mpane. Mpane's work commanded the attention

of all museum-goers. It demanded the sober and present attention of all its viewers. His exhibit, placed in the central point of the museum, was entitled, "Burgeoning Congo." The work was meant to enlighten viewers to the torture that the Congolese people were subjected to due to Belgian colonization and imperialism while inspiring them to have hope for the future of the (now) Democratic Republic of Congo. Mpane's piece was commissioned by the museum to right its original wrong, depicted in the previous "artwork" stationed in the same spot as Mpane's. The former work consisted of bronze statues, situated on pedestal-like structures, lining the walls of the exhibit. These bronze statues were dehumanizing and false depictions of the struggles of the Congolese people during their period of colonization. The pieces were also placed in the center of the museum to glorify the conquests of Leopold II. In the context of a society attempting to classify itself as "post-racial" (for all intents and purposes), the museum decided to devise a plan to undo their decision of displaying the work, to begin with. However, Mpane's masterpiece was far more powerful than I believe the museum had envisioned. Mpane's work consisted of three components: two large wooden statues in the center of the room, and veils lining the walls.

Description and Impact of Aimé Mpane's Exhibit

One of the statues depicted a skull. The skull is a portrayal of former Congolese Chief Lusinga. Chief Lusinga was decapitated in a raid of his village by a Belgian officer in 1884. After being removed from its appropriate location, the skull had been used in Belgian society as a prop, representing Belgian conquest. The veils lining the walls, ironically, and strikingly covered the bronze statues in the room. The fronts of the veils were decorated with printed graphic material. Each veil portrayed the Congolese struggles against imperialism from an authentic and moving perspective. These veils served as a response to the bronze statues. It was as if they declared emphatically, "You didn't win. You could never win because you haven't broken the spirit of the rich country you tried to conquer. The spirit lives on in its descendants, and your legacy will continue to be undone."

The other statue was positioned next to the statue of Chief Lusinga's skull. This other work depicted the head of a Congolese man, who had a bronze palm tree growing from his head as well as bronze pouring from beneath his bust. This symbolized the hope that is growing among the Congolese people. It was a further declaration of the resilience and strength of the Congolese people. For me, this work was a reminder that although many African Americans aren't connected to African countries, we are connected to their peoples because of the similar pain we share, as a byproduct of racism and white supremacy. This work physically moved me and compelled me to catch my breath and my thoughts while in the museum. I was in awe and filled with an immense feeling of gratitude for having been a witness to a quiet, yet powerful revolution.

Revelations, René Magritte, and Self Discovery

In addition, my aunt and I visited The Magritte Museum. Although I had briefly studied the artwork of René Magritte, I was unaware that he considered himself more of a philosopher than an artist. With this same perspective, his art became the vehicle for his philosophical musings. While many people have marveled at his work for its perceived whimsy and surreal nature, his intent behind most of his work was more substantive. In the museum, there were quotes of Magritte's, lined against the wall, above his pieces, providing insight into his creative mindset.

Magritte believed that art needed to provoke conversations about and challenge a viewer's preconceived societal and cultural notions. If those criteria weren't met, Magritte would not consider the work art. He scoffed at pieces done for the sake of luxury. He articulated that they served virtually no purpose because they were bland or completely lacking in substantive meaning. These quotes, along with Magritte's corresponding work, lit a spark within me as an artist. They revitalized my purpose for creating art. I became enthusiastic to create new work upon my arrival back home. However, as the saying goes, "heavy is the head that wears the crown." Upon further reflection of Magritte's statements, I felt the power of art move my spirit. I was compelled to question my artistic intent in past pieces and devise new and informed intent for new pieces.

Final Thoughts

Art, created by humans, holds power because it is living. This trip helped me realize that art that's created, as well as the art in nature and society, are one and the same because they are both living. They repeat each other, they take from each other, and they complete each other. Both forms of art are destined to be immortal. This is because a piece of art or a life experience will always be met with a new perspective, new analysis, or a new approach. This newness is what immortalizes and expands the impact of the work. If life continues to happen, art in all forms will continue to thrive.

DARA SENNAAR (originally from the US) is an undergraduate student at the Earl G. Graves School of Business and Management. Her major is Business Administration. She is double minoring in French and Women, Gender, and Sexuality Studies. Email: dasen1@morgan.edu

5

A Transformational Journey

Katrina L. Pitts, *United States*

There's a sweet, sweet Spirit in this place, and I know that it's the Spirit of the Lord. There are sweet expressions on each face, and I know you feel the presence of the Lord.

When Doris Akers wrote the above lyrics in 1962, she had no idea that in 2004 she would so accurately describe my feelings when I arrived in Kenya, East Africa. This was not only my first journey out of the United States, but it was my first journey to the continent of Africa. I was so excited that I did not realize that it took me a whole day to get there. The journey was an emotional, eye-opening experience for me in several different ways. In the beginning, I did not understand why I was so emotional. However, reflecting on the experience, I began to understand why it captivated my heart. I quickly learned that you cannot believe everything you read and hear about other places, but you must experience them for yourself. Everything that I thought I knew about the people in Africa and their actions were simply not true. I really did not know what to expect from the team that was assigned to guide us on our journey, but the treatment was phenomenal. I made a mental note to return to the country just to see if I would be treated similarly. In other words, myths were shattered; I experienced unimaginable love and kindness, and the experience provided me with a sense of identity that I was lacking as an African American living in the United States.

Myths Shattered

As I reflect on my journey to Kenya, the myths began to shatter as I disembarked the plane and walked into the airport. As I was navigating my way to customs, there was a sense of familiarity. Paying closer attention, I realized that I knew the song playing throughout the airport. It was Usher's *"U Got It Bad."* From that moment, I knew that the experience would be something different, something that I never could have imagined. Over the course of my two-week stay, I experienced so many other things that I did not expect as I explored a country on the other side of the world. The phrase, so close yet so far away, entered my mind many times as a closeness was shared, through popular phrases spoken by the elders to similar beliefs and mannerisms observed.

One of the biggest myths that was shattered was that the people of Africa live in horrid conditions, are poor, and starving. There were high levels of poverty but that simply was not the case for everyone. The images I was used to seeing on television only depicted the most desperate of conditions on the continent of Africa. There were so many beautiful places in Kenya. While there, we were able to visit Mombasa and stayed in a hotel with an ocean view. To see the sunrise coming up over the water each day gave me a sense of paradise. Never would I have imagined such a site based on the images that I had seen about Africa. I visited a huge metropolis (Nairobi), where Africans run governments, businesses, and megachurches. The faces of people that looked like me were even on the currency. Other myths that were shattered are that Africans have a type of animosity toward African Americans, and their perception of us is we are-selfish and entitled. I was also told that it would be difficult to establish any real bonds with the native Africans because there would be a separation between us. I never experienced anyone that seemed to exemplify any such perceptions, which led me to the next revelation.

Love and Kindness Shown
During my visit, I did see many who were in poverty and less fortunate than me, but with what little they had, they were more than willing to share it with me. They offered everything to ensure that I was comfortable, and they were able to take a little and make much. Everywhere we went, people were interested in hearing about my life and my experience as an American. I was more interested in hearing stories about their experiences living in Kenya. At the school we partnered with, one student shared her hopes and dreams of traveling to America to attend college. I shared my passion for gaining more experience as an educator. One of the school's administrators asked if I would be interested in teaching at the school. I was assured those arrangements could be made for me to do so. The gesture alone was enough to warm my heart. We were invited into so many homes and offices of local leaders while there and each was extremely hospitable to our group. They shared stories about the current state of affairs in the area we were visiting and allowed us to interact with the people in the area. They were kind and excited to see people that looked like them who had come from America to visit and

share information. As we discussed our purposes for traveling so far, we heard many heartbreaking stories about some of their experiences. However, through it all, they persevered. Their stories helped me to be more thankful of my circumstances. As I heard about their lived experiences, I couldn't help but marvel at the resilience of the people that I stood before. I think I learned more during this journey than I taught. We went with a mission to teach but I became the actual pupil.

A Sense of Identity

The journey led us to Fort Jesus in Mombasa. The Portuguese built the fort in the 16th century. It became a central location in the East African slave trade. Touring a facility that housed slaves before they were taken from their homeland was a somber experience. Walking the path that led them to ships that would take them to a place of no return was heart wrenching. The tears that flowed from the thoughts of the ordeal were in honor of every person stripped of their right to freedom. These moments penetrated my heart as I thought about my ancestors' forced journey, and the journey had taken their freedom to return. This journey allowed me to see all that my ancestors could have been in their homeland. The things they could have achieved if they were able to live freely. The trip to Fort Jesus remains with me as one of the most significant experiences I have had.

Another experience that had a profound effect on me occurred on a trip to a local market. I was shopping with some other people that were traveling with me when one of the locals approached and asked me where I was from. When I responded that I was American, he stated that he thought that I was local. He stated that I had the features of someone from the Kikuyu tribe. We engaged in a little small talk afterwards; however, his comments about the Kikuyu tribe stuck with me. When we returned to our guides, I was interested in confirming what the gentlemen said to me, so I asked our guides, "If I were Kenyan, what tribe do I look like I am from." Immediately, my guide stated that I looked as if I was Kikuyu. His response provided me with a knowledge that I never had before. It is difficult to not know your true origins. However, that one piece of information allowed me to adopt Kenya as my native land. The comments also gave me a sense of comfort that I never thought was important before.

I had an opportunity to return to Kenya in 2019 for my second journey to Africa. When I arrived, one of our guides greeted us in the airport stating, "Welcome Home." My response was, "It feels good to be home." That sweet, sweet spirit in that place represented the presence of the Lord.

KATRINA L. PITTS is a graduate student in the School of Education and Urban Studies at Morgan State University. Her major research interests lie in the areas of women's empowerment, online learning, experiential education, integrative learning, and career and professional development. Email: pittsk75@gmail.com

6

I Reached My Goal of Earning a PhD through International Study

R. Jerome Anderson, *United States*

In 2000, I was living and working in Armenia. I went there in 1999 to work on land reform projects funded by the United States Agency for International Development. My wife and two youngest children were with me; the three oldest were in various stages of their collegiate careers. One day, I said to my wife, "I would like to get a PhD. I'm thinking of Rutgers or the University of Wisconsin." My wife replied, "You have 3 kids in college. You are NOT quitting your job to return to school." Wives are such spoilsports. You get a good idea, and your wife immediately quashes it.

At the time, I was a licensed attorney, and I tried to keep current with the continuing legal education requirement necessary to maintain my license. The American Bar Association held part of its annual meeting in London that year, so we decided to go to London as a family. My wife and the kids would sightsee; I would attend classes. While we were in London, I somehow (I don't remember how) learned a PhD could be obtained through research at English universities. No classes needed, just write the required number of words (80,000-100,000) and you would receive your doctorate. I was determined to try.

After we returned to Armenia, I wrote a proposal for a PhD research project. My goal was to examine the legal framework for cities in the former Soviet Union. I sent my proposal to three English universities. For various reasons, none of them worked out.

Disappointed but not daunted, I tried again. Before I attended law school, I earned a master's degree in urban planning. I never practiced planning, but I was intrigued by the role of cities as engines of economic growth. Living as I was in Yerevan, the capital of Armenia, I could see the idle factories from the Soviet period and the relative poverty of many Armenians. I wondered how those cities could become engines of economic growth as cities are in other countries. I wrote another proposal, explaining I wished to study the economics of post-socialist cities. I sent that proposal to three schools. Two did not work out, but I did receive an email from Barry Wood, a professor in the School of Architecture, Landscape, and Planning at the University of Newcastle-upon-Tyne. Professor Wood said he found my topic interesting and was willing to supervise my research. In the summer of 2001, I went to Newcastle and met

23

with Barry. Our meeting was fruitful. I submitted my application and began my studies in September 2001.

I was a bit naïve regarding the PhD; in the beginning, I thought it was just a big term paper. Barry told me I needed data. I read and thought and read some more and concluded I would study the backward and forward linkages among industrial firms that drive agglomeration effects and thus urban economic growth. I developed a questionnaire, identified firms to be interviewed, and hired a local sociologist to conduct the interviews. Before my work in Yerevan ended, I had begun to analyze the data. Barry thought the thesis would be strengthened if I conducted the same survey in another post-socialist city. He had a colleague in Sofia, Bulgaria. On my way to my next overseas assignment, I flew to Sofia, met with Barry's colleague, and explored possibilities in Sofia. An official of the Bulgarian Industry Association agreed to conduct the surveys in Sofia. The interviews were successful, and I had data from two cities.

I wrote the dissertation in the various countries in which I worked during the six years it took to complete it. I began it in Armenia and wrote various parts of it in Amman, Jordan; Baghdad, Iraq; various cities in the former Yugoslavia; Faizabad and Kabul, Afghanistan; and at home in suburban Washington, DC. I finished the dissertation in May 2007, defended it successfully in July, and was awarded the PhD in August 2007, one month shy of my 58th birthday. It was an arduous six-year journey, but it was well worth it. The PhD gave a needed boost to my career.

But more important than the boost to my career was the way it changed me. Much of the reading I did for my thesis was by European authors. While I had worked internationally since 1992 and had an international perspective, reading works of European authors made me even more aware of the differences in thinking between many in Europe and many in the United States. I value the perspective of those from the other side of the "pond." I do not have a United States-centric perspective. I see the world differently and am grateful I do. Earning the degree from an English university made that possible. My wife was correct in telling me I could not quit my job and go to either Rutgers or Wisconsin. I was much better for studying in England.

The other change that I value is the way I learned to think. Earning a PhD means learning to think in much more rigorous ways. When I worked in Afghanistan after completing the PhD, I could tell the difference between the advisors who had master's degrees and those who had doctorates. There was a noticeable difference in their thinking, and many times I thought those with only a master's degree really did not know how to analyze a problem properly or deeply. I may have become an intellectual snob to a certain degree but doing the work to earn a doctorate does change a person's way of thinking. The conferral of that degree can, and does, make one a different person. I value that.

As meaningful as the PhD experience was, it was not the end of my international education. From March 2013 through September 2015 I worked in Monrovia,

Liberia. While there I enrolled in an online master's degree program from the University of Illinois at Chicago. By day I worked as the Concessions Advisor, helping various agencies of the Liberian government improve the way they managed natural resource concessions. By nights and on weekends I studied measurement, evaluation, statistics, and assessment, and was awarded the M.Ed. degree in August 2015, eight years after completing the PhD and six weeks before I left Liberia. That degree enabled me to transition to work in the United States, as I ended my international consulting career when I returned from Liberia. Thus, international education has benefited me in numerous ways throughout much of my life. International education has given me skills I needed professionally, and a perspective on the world I value. I would not be the person I am without my two degrees earned in international education.

R. JEROME ANDERSON is a doctoral student in the Urban Educational Leadership Program in the School of Education and Urban Studies at Morgan State University in Baltimore, MD. His research concerns academic achievement of minority students in Maryland's urban school districts. Email: roand4@morgan.edu

7

The Semester of My Dreams in Madrid, Spain

Janice Alonzo, *United States*

During the summer between third and fourth grade, we were given the opportunity to participate in a Spanish-language program at our elementary school. Growing up in white middle class suburban Syracuse, New York in the 1980s and 1990s, we did not have much exposure or contact with people of other cultures, languages, or racial backgrounds, so I jumped at the chance. Syracuse was a great place to grow up; I had amazing teachers and friends and participated in the band and many extracurricular activities. My parents were especially supportive of anything I did and wanted to pursue, as they were public school teachers and wanted to give me and my brother every opportunity that existed in the world.

The Beginning of My Thirty-Five Year Love for Spanish
When this summer Spanish program was advertised, I immediately asked my parents if I could join, and they said yes. I remember walking in the first day and learning that "miércoles" means Wednesday. I could not believe that there were other words for the days of the week. I was hooked and enthralled, and I never wanted to stop learning Spanish from that day forward. I took Spanish throughout middle school and all four years of high school, and I also took the Spanish AP exam. As I studied more and more about the different Spanish accents, capital cities, traditional food, and more, I made my goal in college to study abroad in Madrid, Spain. I did not want to go anywhere else but Madrid. The capital city of Spain--home to centuries of history and relationships with Africa and the Middle East as well as the rest of Europe. Home to Placido Domingo and Lope de Vega. Home to the Real Madrid soccer team and Las Ventas bullfighting ring.

After high school, I attended Ithaca College (New York). I applied to and was accepted to the Ithaca-in-Madrid program and spent a semester in this amazing capital city in the fall of 1997 which was my junior year. Every correspondence from Ithaca in the summer leading up to that semester (information about my host family, plane tickets, class schedule, orientation, etc.) made my heartbeat faster. To this day, I still say that the fall of 1997 was the best time of my life until my son was born twenty years later in 2017.

It was also the year that Princess Diana died in the terrible car accident in Paris. One of the first impressions I had of my host mother Feliciona ("Feli") was of her crying the whole day of Diana's funeral. Feli's kids, Rafa and Maria, were in the living room too, and my roommate and I just sat with them for what seemed like hours watching the funeral and talking about Diana and her family. We bonded that day, and although it was over something tragic, it made us close from the start.

Many of my classmates would travel on the weekends to Portugal, France, Italy, and other places in Europe, but I wanted to stay "home" in Madrid and be a real "Madrileño" walking in Parque Retiro on Sundays and eating Feli's paella with her family. I did homework outside in the courtyard of our apartment building and played with the little kids. My roommate and I would venture to El Corte Inglés or Zara to go shopping, or we would explore a local market. We saw Real Madrid play and saw U2 in concert. It was also here that I became the biggest fan of Ricky Martin when we saw him perform in Las Ventas. My Spain scrapbook still contains pieces of what I call "Ricky Glitter" (silver confetti that was thrown from the stage that night).

I think about my time in Madrid every day; not a day goes by that I am not reminded of my time there or think about people or places in that incredible magical city. When my mom picked me up from the airport that December, she did not even recognize me and said that I matured and grew up to be a self-assured, independent person in just one semester. I saved everything from that semester too. From printouts of emails to my friends and family to tickets to concerts, flyers for events at discotecas, the Ithaca-in-Madrid end-of-semester dinner program, and brochures from places we visited. Everything is in my scrapbook, and every photo is chronologically placed in photo albums that I bought there. Even though I don't fit into my Hard Rock Café Madrid black t-shirt anymore or the light green sweater I bought at Zara, they still sit in my closet with all of my other clothes. I can't part with them.

Madrid's Impact on My Life
Since 1997, I have traveled to 29 countries in my never-ending quest to become more of a global citizen. My mom is my main travel partner, and my preschooler will be our new travel partner as we strive to visit every

country that we can possibly go to in this post-pandemic world. I have taught Spanish 101 and have tutored many students in Spanish, and I have also taught a Global Studies 101 course. At my current job, I translate Spanish for Latino students and their families. I have been a staff member/chaperone on Alternative Break college student trips to Costa Rica and Nicaragua. I have also lived in two states since graduating college, and before I decided to go to graduate school, I didn't even visit the school or the city before going. I knew I would be okay living anywhere new because of my semester spent in Madrid.

While at Ithaca, I earned my B.A. in Anthropology and minored in Spanish. I went on to attend Florida State University and earned my M.A. in International Affairs, and I am currently a doctoral candidate in Morgan State University's Community College Leadership program. My dissertation is the culmination of all my academic and professional experiences, as well as my time in Madrid, as I am focusing on experiences of Spanish-speaking international student-athletes who attend community colleges.

Studying abroad is the absolute best thing anyone can do in college. None of my high school friends or college friends decided to study abroad. None. I feel enriched beyond belief to have studied and spent time away from home and from everything that was familiar to me. I learned how to function on my own and ask questions in another language and not be afraid to meet people from around the world. I was independent and free, and I was proud of living on my own without my family or friends back home. I could do what I wanted to do, and I had to make decisions that sometimes seemed right and sometimes seemed wrong.

Almost every night now, I read a book to my son called "Wherever You Go" by Pat Zietlow Miller (2015) that talks about roads and what you will experience when you leave your house and "just open your door." I smile to myself (and maybe shed a tear too) when I read these passages: "Roads...grow... Which path should I choose? That's easy to see. The one that will take you where you wish to be" and "Roads... remember. Every life landmark, the big and the small. The moments you tripped, the times you stood tall. Where you are going, and where you began. What you expected. What you didn't plan." My semester in Madrid was one of my biggest life landmarks, and I took the road that led to where I wanted to be. There were some expected emotions and experiences but some that no one could plan. I hope I can teach my son that stepping out of his comfort zone is one of the most important things that someone can do to grow as a person.

JANICE ALONZO (originally from the U.S.) is a doctoral student in the Community College Leadership Program in the School of Education and Urban Studies. Her major research interests lie in the areas of international student retention, community college student-athletes, and Latino/a persistence in higher education. Email: jagun2@morgan.edu

8

A Tale of a New City

Sierra DeLoatch, *United States*

High school can be a make-or-break period for a lot of teenagers. It's quite simple, you either sink or you float, and those that fit the gray area in-between are far and few. Well, for me, high school was a place where I didn't float, I soared. I was on the soccer team at school along with a travel team in the county, so I was popular. I was in a special program that allowed me to take honors classes where I easily excelled, and I landed a spot as the key witness in our Mock Trial Club. I was easily and quickly finding who I believed I wanted to be for the next four years of my life, so imagine my dismay when my father ripped it all away.

My hometown in southern Maryland was a haven for me, and Maryland had always been my life. I was comfortable where I was, and I was under the impression that none of that would be changing. My father had just received his assignment from the State Department that he was to go to Israel, and while he was gone the rest of our family would stay home like we had always done. However, after visiting Israel to see the country and discovering the life it had to offer for our family, my father made the executive decision that we were going with him. We were set to depart at the end of June, which would give us time to settle in, do a bit of sight-seeing and adjust to the time difference just before school began. My younger sister jumped at the opportunity. She was excited to embark on this new journey and experience living overseas, but I simply did not want to leave my life behind. I couldn't leave my life behind. I knew I'd be forgotten by my peers; I wouldn't be able to grow in the Mock Trial Club or make the varsity soccer team, but most importantly I had to start over. Looking back now, I know I was blinded by living "the American Dream" my entire life, but at 14 and with clear plans on how I envisioned my future, this was the most devastating thing that could ever happen. The months leading up to the big move were agonizing, each day a constant reminder that I had to leave the life I loved behind and start anew in a literal foreign place. Finally, the big day came, and my life as I knew it would change in ways I would never expect.

A New Beginning

After a 14-hour flight from JFK to Tel Aviv, we finally arrived. This was it, our new lives, our new home, all in a new country. From the moment we landed I told myself that in no way would I ever enjoy this experience, nor would I ever stop protesting my being there. I spent countless nights either crying or pulling all-nighters to talk to my friends from home due to the 7-hour time difference, and I would fake sickness sometimes to stay home from school. Nonetheless, I knew I could not go on living like this for the next year, so I eventually started to give Israel a shot.

First, I found out the school had its own soccer team, and they just so happened to be looking for a goalkeeper. I then found out that not only did the team travel around Israel for away games, but for the end of the year tournament all players had the opportunity to be chosen as a special travel team to a different country to compete. I was in awe. Our school also had a "Week Without Walls" where we could choose where, based on certain programs, we wanted to travel to learn about the culture and history of Israel. I also had joined the Spanish club, where we were planning a trip to Spain in November, and by Christmas, only 6 months after moving, I had already visited 3 new countries. I was still homesick and begged my parents to let us travel home for Christmas, and while I loved being back home, I also discovered that I missed my new home as well.

Year Two
The New Year brought new opportunities, new travel plans, and most importantly brought me only 6 months away from going home. Dad had told us we would only be there for a year, so I knew in June when we left for the summer there was no turning back. Dad also waited for our spring break trip to Turkey to give the news that we would be staying for a second year, and while I was upset, I was also a bit relieved. We finished the rest of the school year and spent the summer back in Maryland visiting family, and touring colleges before my junior year of high school. For years I had been looking forward to one day becoming a lawyer, but after our time abroad I had decided that I wanted to study international affairs, follow my dad's footsteps, and continue to travel the world. I also started looking for schools that would allow me to study abroad in Israel. I had gone from pure hatred of our new home to becoming tolerant and making my life less miserable while we were there, but also planning to return even after we left.

I took our second year in Israel by storm. This is not to say that I had completely overcome my homesickness, but I learned that I could either miss out on and waste a once in a lifetime opportunity or I could take full advantage of it. I became more involved in different clubs; I continued to play sports; I traveled, and I even started learning Hebrew. I fell in love with traveling and the open access I had to do so; I fell in love with my new life as a diplomat, and I fell in love with Israel and all she had to offer me. Our second year flew by too fast, and before I knew it the life that I had come to know and become comfortable living was ripped from under me, just as it had been when I received that fateful news two years prior. No matter how much I tried to hate her, Israel had grown on me. I promised myself I would be back whether that be as a study abroad student or hopefully one day as the American Ambassador for the U.S. Embassy, and while I have already checked off one on my list, the latter remains a long-term goal.

31

A Tale of a New City

The girl that once cried herself to sleep every night from homesickness became the first African American to win Prom Princess in the history of the school. She won MVP and All-Tournament in London for softball and MVP in Belgium for soccer. She traveled to at least 9 different countries in a span of 2 years. She made new friends across the globe, found a passion in learning languages, and even had come to love what she most feared. The most important lesson that she learned, however, was that change was not always bad and she could not continue to allow her life to revolve solely around the United States because there was so much more of the world to explore.

One of our many family adventures, riding camels in Egypt with my sister Courtney (left) and my Uncle Kevin

Those two years I spent living in Israel were not easy. I argued with my parents; I tried to purposely fail classes in hopes they would send me home; I suffused myself so deeply in misery my family eventually ignored it due to how insufferable I was. Now, looking back, I'm so glad they did. I didn't understand then the importance of living abroad, but every day I silently thank my dad for dragging me on one of the best experiences of my life. Not only was I living in one of the most controversial countries in the Middle East, but my father worked in the U.S. Embassy, and we would travel to Jordan, Syria, and even Palestine. This time in my life was when I decided that I no longer wanted to be a lawyer. The more I traveled while living abroad, the more I fell in love with the world. I took interest in international relations and foreign affairs all while I was living through it. Living in Israel and traveling was only a prerequisite in my preparation for one day becoming a graduate student, merely an internship before applying my knowledge to the real world. The courses that I completed during undergrad allowed me to understand through the classroom and real time news international issues pertaining to governance, security, and diplomacy. Now, not only do I possess a real-life experience of seeing how international relations has directly affected the area I lived in, but I also hold a degree that will allow me to further my interests and make a career out of something I am passionate about. Living in Israel created the woman I am today. She opened my eyes to a world beyond the Chesapeake Bay and Atlantic Ocean, and if it wasn't for my time in Israel, I have no idea where I would be today.

SIERRA G. DELOATCH is an American graduate student (MA) in international studies in the College of Liberal Arts. Her major research interests lie in international relations, foreign affairs, and foreign cultures and languages. Email: sidel1@morgan.edu

9

Unique Experiences Through Study Abroad

Samala B. Lewis, *United States*

I grew up in Baltimore, Maryland in the United States. Baltimore City is a very urban area, and it is filled with many opportunities to explore. However, one of the most unique and spiritual experiences was not experienced in my lovely hometown. This unique spiritual experience occurred in Dominica, West Indies. I was blessed to live in Dominica for 2.5 years as a medical student at Ross University School of Medicine.

Study Abroad

My experience in Dominica as a medical student was a beautiful experience. There were students from all over the world at the school. Most of the students came from different religious, cultural, and economic backgrounds than me and from each other. Despite these differences, all of us were sharing the same human experience of being away from our families in a new country tackling new challenges. Students connected on this shared human experience, and this melting pot of student cultures, views, and belief systems helped put me on a path to think and be successful in a global capacity.

Building Relationships

I met many friends during this experience, with whom I am still in touch 15 years later. One experience with a dear friend tops the list as one of my most spiritual experiences of all time. We were able to bond over this unique experience. During certain times of the year, brush fires were frequent, and firemen would bravely manage the brush fires. One day after visiting Fort Shirley, my diverse group of new friends decided to take a walk through the beautiful country. We noticed that the air was very warm and saw the glow of a brush fire higher up the mountain.

Kindness from Others

A firetruck pulled beside us to inform us that a brush fire was in the area, and to give us a ride if we needed it. Through friendly discussion, the firemen learned that we were all students studying abroad, and we all conversed about the beautiful country. The brush fire was a safe distance away and we all stood on top of the fire truck. The feeling was so peaceful and amazing.

Conclusion

It was a beautiful and serene experience that heightened the senses. You could feel the warming wind, which was blowing more than usual, on your face, skin and blowing through your hair. You could smell and see smoke in the air. We could see small pieces of red ash in the air. The red ash turned black and grey as it blew closer to us and landed on out skin, hair, and clothes. The view was so beautiful and serene that no one cared about the ash on our skin, hair, and clothes.

Samala Lewis, Joy'l Thomas and Christina Weisenborn (Co-Editors)

We all just watched, laughed, and took in the beauty of the moment. We all knew that this was a once in a lifetime experience. Luckily, just as the ash started coming down too thick and just as the air became too smoky, the warm rain began to fall, making the moment even more beautiful. I have seen many beautiful sites in my life, but none as beautiful as this. If not for the study around experience, I may have missed out on this beautiful experience.

SAMALA B. LEWIS is a Biology Instructor and the lead professor for Fundamentals of Biology at Carroll Community College. She is also a doctoral candidate in Science Education, conducting research on the Multicultural Teaching Competency and use of Culturally Relevant Educational Practices of Science Teachers. Samala has completed scientific research in environmental science to control harmful algal blooms and molecular biology on the causes of neural tube defects in zebrafish. Email: slewis4@carrollcc.edu

10

Ghana as the Gateway to International Travel

Fawaz Abdullah, *United States*

I am originally from Baltimore, Maryland. My mother is from Accra, Ghana while my father is from Camden, New Jersey. I like to think that I came from the best of both worlds. As an African American, my heritage is traced back to Africa, the land from which we black people originated. My father is from America, the land of opportunity; therefore, I am a true African American. I have been to my mother's home country in Accra, Ghana three times, and each time I stayed for three to five months. For the first-time visiting Ghana, my parents sent me with my aunt because she was traveling to Ghana, and they did not want me to miss the opportunity. My last two visits were with my mother and my two younger sisters. Africa and America are very different. One obvious difference is the language.

During my time in Africa, I learned to speak and understand one of the native languages called Hausa. I learned this language by observing and listening. Unfortunately, I forgot how to speak Hausa fluently, and now I can only say little words and phrases, but I understand what someone is saying in Hausa and can translate it (if that makes sense). Another difference is the money exchange. Ghanaian money is called a Cedi, and one Cedi is worth sixteen cents in American money. I was delighted that my American money would buy me more goods in Ghana than in America.

The food in Ghana is also very different from the food in America. In Ghana, we ate food such as Jollof, which is a rice dish, peanut butter soup which is made with real peanut butter, Groundnut soup, and a soup called Iyoyo, which is made with greens such as spinach and other green leaves. These soups/stews are gravies for FuFu, which is similar to Jell-O because of how floppy it is, Dakunu which is somewhat like FuFu but stiffer, and rice. Other dishes that I ate, but was not fond of, were Dundu which is similar to potatoes, and Wakey, beans and rice.

Another strange and unusual difference I saw was women walking throughout the neighborhood streets carrying large bowls on their heads that contained their merchandise for selling different items such as sugarcane, my favorite, coconuts, and other edible delicacies. Women also carried their babies wrapped in a sheet on their backs instead of pushing them in strollers like American women. Scattered among these women were loose animals, like chickens, roosters, goats, and sheep roaming around the same neighborhood streets. These animals belonged to different people, but the people in the neighborhood knew who owned the animals.

During my second time visiting Ghana, I attended elementary school. The schools there were different from schools in America in terms of discipline. Perhaps not all the schools were the same, but the school I attended was very strict. If students misbehaved or were disrespectful, the teachers had permission to physically discipline them but in a non-abusive manner. In American schools, the policy is "hands-off" no matter what!

Though there were many differences, there were some similarities. In Ghana, there were barbershops with professional barbers, like the neighborhood shops in America. Conveniently there was a barbershop outside our house where I would go, to get a haircut that was on point, like my barber would cut my hair in America. Whenever I looked at myself in the mirror I grinned with happiness. There were also cars, buses, big houses, motorcycles, restaurants serving Ghanaian and American food, and other buildings essential to people's lives. There was a beach that we would always visit on Sundays, and on Saturdays, we would always go to the Accra Mall. My mother arranged it so that my sisters and I would go to the mall with her trusted friend's son, so we could look forward to something fun at the end of the week, even though every time we went, we bought nothing except food.

Throughout the week, my mother took us to different places in Accra, so we could meet her friends and explore the city, which was very exciting. The beach, however, was my favorite experience because I celebrated a birthday. The whole family in Ghana got together, and we all went to the beach to celebrate my birthday; it was awesome. At the time, I was about eight years old, and seeing the ocean for the first time and riding the horses on the beach was thrilling and made that birthday celebration one that I would always remember.

Overall, I loved my experience in Ghana, and I hope to visit there again. Also, I have to talk with my Ghanaian uncle Ali, who lives in Japan and has a Japanese family, to arrange a visit to Japan. I want to take my future wife and children to Japan someday and show them a good time just like I had in Ghana.

FAWAZ ABDULLAH is a freshman student enrolled at Morgan State University in the School of Engineering. I aspire to be a successful electrical engineer and graduate within four years with a bachelor's degree in engineering. I want to also help my community and continue to be a role model for my community. E-mail: faabd9@morgan.edu

11
Travel through Association

Keivon Anderson, *United States*

I am an international student even though I've never stepped foot off the east coast of the United States. Even though I've never been to Guam or Dubai like Bradley, or I wasn't born in Poland like Jacob, and unlike Drew, my dad doesn't like to spend the summer on his beach home in the Caribbean. Despite not being able to say I have ties outside the United States, I still understand what it is like to submerge yourself in an unfamiliar setting. The names I mentioned were those of my classmates in high school. Believe it or not, most of my other classmates were like Bradley, Jacob, and Drew. White, privileged, and well-off. Very much, "Country Club." I, however, was the exact opposite. I was Black, middle-class, blue-collar. I wasn't the only Black kid at my school, but they were scarce. A lot of times, I was the only person of color in my classes. Because of this, I began to learn more about upper-class culture. Hearing stories about yachts and business meetings, only the bourgeoisie could tell. I, however, couldn't even count on a summer vacation.

Eventually, I learned the lingo of my classmates, and began to understand the inner workings of a white teenager, and what privilege is. Through this, I was able to communicate and even relate to my classmates. Likewise, my classmates began to learn about my culture, and I started to tell them stories of the middle class. I spent four years at my luxurious private school, and I was able to learn more about the world than just my neighborhood.

Like I said, even though I've never been to Guam or Dubai like Bradley, or I wasn't born in Poland like Jacob, and unlike Drew, my dad doesn't like to spend the summer on his beach home in the Caribbean. Instead, I've been to Towson, Maryland.

KEIVON ANDERSON is an undergraduate student with a sociology major at Morgan State University. E-mail: keand16@gmail.com

12

Similarities Are Greater than Differences

Dale Plater, *The Bahamas*

There is nothing quite like the experience of connecting with someone else's culture and completely immersing yourself in it for years. The culture shock that comes with it is immense and makes you reflect on the differences between your culture and theirs. When I was ten my parents got divorced and then when I was twelve my mother remarried. My stepfather is from the island of Nassau located in The Bahamas; he was the Deputy Chief Medical Officer at the Ministry of Health. He had a very important job so we all gladly moved to Nassau so he could continue to work and so we could all experience culture as well.

When I first moved there, I had trouble adjusting to the new atmosphere I was introduced to. People spoke with a dialect that I was not used to which made it difficult to hold conversations or even talk to people at all. When other students found out I was new they taught me how people spoke and what certain things meant to help me better understand people. Even with the help of my classmates, I still felt like it was hard to fit in with everyone. The schools there also start at first grade and go all the way up to twelfth grade unlike schools in America that make you switch schools for elementary school, middle school, and high school. Most of my classmates had been at my school since they started school altogether which means friendships had groups had already been established long before I arrived. Students would talk to me and ask me things about America and compare certain things there like our school systems, fast food restaurants, and other things, but it still did not feel like I was truly making friends. Around a month after school started, I found a common interest in things with some students that none of us thought to talk about. We all spent so much time talking about the things that made us different that divided us that we did not realize the things we had in common. We had similar tastes in music, video games, and even content creators that we all liked. Once we started talking about things that made us similar, I began to open up more and more and eventually became comfortable around people.

Once I opened up more, I was ready to fully immerse myself in my new life on the island and a good starting point was an event called Junkanoo which was vastly approaching. Junkanoo is a street parade where people dress up in costumes and dance and play music. That year my family and I participated and had such a great time. My brother and I played drums with our parents and marched with the groups all night. It was something else that brought me closer to people and gave me a better understanding and in-depth look at their culture. Although there are many street parades in America there is nothing quite like Junkanoo which is rooted in African culture and history. It is still to this day one of the most notable differences between America and The Bahamas.

My Family and I participating in Junkanoo

When the time for high school came around, I ended up switching schools and had to make new friends. Just like last time people asked me about the differences between America and The Bahamas and while telling them I also added in similarities which showed them that while I may be a little different not that much different than them. I had an easier time making friends and found people who I think I can consider lifelong friends.

Overall my time in The Bahamas really helped to shape and define the person I have become today. I learned that although there might be many cultural differences between you and someone else, that shouldn't stop you from learning about their culture. Even though we have our differences, we aren't all that different from one another.

DALE PLATER is an undergraduate student in the Fine Arts Department at Morgan State University. His major is graphic design with a plan to receive a Master's Degree in Art History. Email: dapla2@morgan.edu

13

Internationally Non-Traditional

Dominique Turner, *United States*

So, what are we doing here? I vividly recall that moment when I finally understood how we were administering the Office of International Programs and I was left with the glaring question, "So what are we doing here?" No F1 visas. No onsite courses. No direct contact with students. Institution-to-institution partnerships only… So, what are we doing here? A more suitable question might have been, "Why are we doing this this way?" From my first day on the job, I understood WHAT we were doing. But it took some time to understand WHY we were doing what we were doing in the manner in which we were doing it.

According to Skinner (2020), the term foreign student was the precursor to international student. Traces of the term foreign student can be seen as far back as the 1980's. Although the two terms were synonymous at one point, they are now distinct concepts. Clark (2009) indicates that an international student refers to "students crossing borders for the specific purpose of studying". Additionally, Clark (2009) defines foreign students as "non-citizens enrolled at an institution of education outside their home country, but who have not necessarily crossed a border to study." The important distinction to note between these two terms is somewhat minimal and awkward to identify. The difference is related to the individual's reason for relocating to a new country. A foreign student could have moved to a country outside of their country of citizenship for a purpose other than pursuing college initially, but then decided later to attend college. The international student, on the other hand, relocates to a new country for the specific purpose of going to college.

But what should we make of the international student who never leaves her or his home country? Does the lack of international travel eliminate a student from having an international learning experience? While this type of international student is a bit non-traditional, these experiences should not be invalidated. As we continue to experience the intersection of globalization and technological advancement (or maybe technology convergence) we will likely see an increase in new types of experience among international students that require more technological involvement and less physical travel.

All of this information adds a great deal of context to my journey as Director of International Programs at the University of Maryland Global Campus (UMGC), a state online university. This duality makes the university's institutional identity a bit complicated. While there is a rich culture that values being part of the University System of Maryland, there is also a strategic mandate to compete with for-profit colleges and universities in the online higher education space. This clash in culture and strategy impacts how the university has structured its Office of International Programs. The university attempts to balance the desire to identify new sources of revenue with the opportunity to increase the university's global reach through prestigious academic partnerships through the Office of International Programs.

The major hurdle to administering an online international program from my experience has been communication. There are countless stories that my colleagues and I could share about how difficult it has been to collaborate with a language barrier, a time difference, and having never heard one another's voice. I vividly recall a rather explosive exchange between my office and my counterpart at an institution with which we have an international programs partnership in Russia. I spent several months sending emails that were never answered requesting signatures on the renewal paperwork. Six months after my initial email, our communication reached a boiling point when I received an email in bold red letters and multiple exclamation points indicating that the matter was "now urgent" and that I should implore the senior leadership of my university to sign new copies of the paperwork again. The email went on to suggest that I had not sent repeated emails over the six-month period requesting attention to this matter. After taking some time to calm down and ensure that I had not imagined sending six months' worth of emails, I drafted and sent a very professional and diplomatic email that made my requests very clear, communicated the offensive nature of the email that was sent to me, and requested a video conference to discuss the path forward. The response from my Russian counterpart was very apologetic and the tone much softer than her previous message. She went on to say that my predecessor at UMGC who spoke fluent Russian and was well-versed in Russian culture would tell her that, "Russians sometimes sound rude when they worry too much about a problem". She explained the scenario from her perspective, and we used the issue to improve our communication and strengthen the partnership between our universities.

While there are other examples, this scenario is an excellent representation of the difficulty in communicating while administering a fully online international program. The COVID-19 pandemic continues to devastate the higher education industry and force institutions to rethink their approach to international ventures. Universities have canceled study abroad and made substantial modifications to international student services amid government guidance on international travel. Additionally, colleges are increasing online and offer hybrid courses. Each of these indicators point to a potential increase in the non-traditional approach to international programs UMGC. If this model does gain some traction in higher education, international programs administrators will need a commitment to professionalism, respect for cultural differences, and the patience to learn from international colleagues toward the goal of strong partnerships.

DOMINIQUE TURNER (originally from the United States) is a doctoral student in the Higher Education Administration Program in the School of Education and Urban Studies. His major research interests lie in the area of governance in high education, history of higher education, and graduate student services. Email: dotur6@morgan.edu

14

In the Kingdom

Jameeka Michelle Gillis, *United States*

Born and raised in the United States of America, I have been able to travel to many states, as well as to other countries. Even with all the traveling I have done in my life, I had never crossed the Atlantic Ocean.

In the Eastern Hemisphere
In the summer of 2017, I was given the opportunity to go to the Kingdom of Cambodia for two weeks. I went to this beautiful kingdom as a volunteer to teach English to elementary school age children. My older sister came with me. For the two weeks that we were there, we were housed in a boarding dormitory with several other volunteers. Our meals were provided, cooked, and prepared by the volunteer cooking staff.

In the town
On our first day in the kingdom, we were taken on a tour of the Tuol Sleng Genocide Museum. This museum focuses on a key part of Cambodia's history—the genocide of the darker skinned Cambodians. This old schoolhouse was turned into a security prison from 1975-1979 and is now a historical museum. The history given to us on that first day was both rich and sad.

Along with the museum visit, we, the volunteers, were taken on a tour of the city where we were staying, Phnom Penh. We went to the market, which was an open-air street market. This was a new experience for me. I did, however, jump at the chance to get some street food, which was delicious.

In the school
On our first workday, the volunteers were taken to their different school locations to meet the staff and students. Everyone was friendly. Being that I am slightly disabled, walking with a walker, I found many people to be extremely helpful to me. The children were excited to meet their new teachers. The principal, or lead teacher, saw my difficulty with using the many steps in the building and decided to make accommodations for me.

So, after meeting my students, I was given a different task to complete for my two-week stay. I was now in charge of developing curriculum material and lesson plans that would cover the students' class time for a period of a few months.

This was a great task that my sister and I tackled with grace. We, for the first time in our lives, worked as a team; and I was the leader. The principal provided me with the template, and I created different learning goals and assignments for the students to achieve and complete. As a result of not being able to travel to the school, my sister and I stayed in the dorm for most of our time in Cambodia. We got to know the Cambodian volunteers really well because of this.

In my mind
From traveling across the world and living and working there, I learned to, first, appreciate the opportunities that I had in my life. Being able to travel and volunteer was a big feat for me. Being able to do this with a loved one made this time even more special. I learned that I was truly capable of doing anything that I put my mind to, even with having a slight disability. I am able.

Jameeka Michelle Gillis *(originally from the United States of America)* is a doctoral student in the English program at Morgan State University. Her major research interests include language and professional writing and African American literature. E-mail: jagil1@morgan.edu

15

Culture Shock in My Culture

Jennifer Dasilva-Hassiman, *Venezuela*

I was born in Caracas, Venezuela. I lived there until I was 7-years old. I jumped at the opportunity when my dean announced that he was hosting a Fulbright Hays in Colombia. Beyond having a chance to immerse myself in the Colombian culture and learn about the peace conflict, I thought of all the nostalgic memories I would be able to recreate due to the proximity shared both geographically and culturally between Colombia and Venezuela.

I'm heading back home

Prior to arriving in Colombia, I was full of excitement. "This study abroad is going to be a breeze; I know everything about the culture, and it'll be like going back home for a few weeks," I said to myself. In my mind there was not much I had to learn about the culture, rather I would be learning about the Colombian peace conflict and the way the mass migration from Venezuela was impacting Colombian society. At first, my family had some reservations regarding my trip due to safety concerns, but once they saw my excitement they quickly got on board.

In shock

While preparing for the trip, I had my head held high with a "know it" attitude thinking I would be a guide to all the other group members. I felt as though I would be fully embraced by the Colombian people since I came from a similar culture. Once I got there, I was shocked, everything looked so different from what I remembered. Despite me never having visited Colombia, I thought it would feel like home. Everything hit me at once, all the childhood memories I had of Venezuela were faint. I don't remember much about the seven years living there but I do remember spending my summer vacations there visiting my family that stayed behind. I had fun-filled, luxurious, and eventful memories of Venezuela because when we would visit, we would stay at high-end hotels or resort types of lodging. I could not believe how different everything was, nothing was the same. I was accustomed to the 'First World' luxuries associated with living in the United States. I was often asked what certain things meant or what people were saying by my colleagues and through embarrassing situations and awkward encounters. I came to find out my Spanish wasn't as sharp as I thought.

Living in America for twenty years changed me more than I thought. When my family and I first moved to America my father only allowed us to speak English in the house so that we would learn the language quicker. I never realized how many words/phrases I had forgotten. The overwhelming feeling was unbearable. I could not believe the level of shock I experienced. On one of the days in Bogota I remember paying for an empanada, I accidentally gave the empanada man, a Venezuelan native, extra money due to the difference in currency, he laughed at the simple mistake and asked where in the United States I was from. Although the empanada man who was meant it as an innocent joke everything hit me hard at that moment. I took immense pride in the fact that I was the only one on the trip who was from South America and would not be in culture shock. The fact that a Venezuelan native did not embrace me as one of his own was unanticipated.

Stepping back

After taking a moment to gather my thoughts and having a talk with myself and my father back at home, I decided that it was ok to not know everything. It was fine that the trip was not going as I planned. Rather, my father persuaded me to focus on all the learning possibilities. Aside from freshening up on my Spanish, I had the chance to learn about new cultures, indigenous traditions, the peace conflict, and most importantly I had a chance to learn all these notions firsthand rather than reading about them through my textbooks. My entire mindset changed; I had a chance to learn about the topics I read about from the people who experienced them. My brain switched from teacher mode to student mode. The information, lessons, and experiences I was able to digest were invaluable.

There were classes every day and multiple topics covered daily. They were all pivotal in understanding Colombian history, conflict, and culture. The first couple of weeks were focused on survivors of the war. Hearing first-hand accounts of war survivors was an emotional experience. Coming from and living in the United States I always thought of war as this violent act that occurs in faraway places. It was a complete shock to hear the stories of people who not only lived through it but were also dealing with the aftermath during these current times. Topics such as restorative justice came about. You could hear the pain in peoples' voices who questioned how there can be peace without proper justice. In essence, there were a lot of mixed feelings regarding the government's handling of the ex-Revolutionary Armed Forces of Colombia (RAFC) leaders. Coming into the study abroad I thought of how happy the people must be because the war against the FARC was technically over. Through listening and inquiring I came to understand that many survivors are not happy with the government's handling of ex-members of the group. Numerous members did not have to serve prison time or pay for the atrocities committed under the government deal; this enraged the survivors who lived through the conflict.

Getting back into the classroom

Aside from learning about the peace process and conflict, I had a chance to visit local Colombian schools and engage with the students through English courses.

Despite arriving as a teacher prepared to teach them basic English phrases, it was I who learned from them. The kids taught me about their personal stories, culture, and future goals. The kids also taught me about their life at home, and some spoke about the struggles they faced. To say the least, it was a humbling experience. I felt instant gratification for all the material things and luxuries I have. Things such as running water and a functional bathroom seemed like an abstract concept for some of the children. I felt so grateful and dumbfounded at the same time. Topics such as environmental justice more specifically the privatization of water, food deserts, and lack of access to healthy air are topics I consider a basic human right but seemed to be a faraway dream to some of the kids.

These issues motivated me to further research. I decided to conduct research regarding the need to mitigate environmental justice issues in a world striving to tackle climate change. I argued that both are synonymous and that we cannot tackle one without the other. I also argued that although the fight against climate change is pivotal on an international level, we must not fail to address the environmental justice issues occurring in marginalized communities. This mind-blowing, emotional, and enriching study abroad experience motivated me to write a children's e-book regarding the peace conflict. My study abroad experiences in Colombia utterly changed how I view my life in all aspects. It allowed me to fully integrate myself into a culture that I hold near and dear to my heart. I am extremely grateful that I had this amazing opportunity.

--
JENNIFER DASILVA-HASSIMAN graduated from Morgan State University in the Spring of 2020. Her major research interests lie in International Studies with a focus on Foreign Policy and Politics in Latin America and the Caribbean. Email: jedas1@morgan.edu

PART II

Experiences of International Students in the United States

16

My International Experience in the United States

Abisola Arowolaju, *Nigeria*

Growing up in the western part of Nigeria, as a child I always thought I had everything easy. I came from an average family of six children, and I am the second of them all. Eighty-five percent of Nigeria's population, especially the youth, feels the urge to escape from the country typically because of her economy, and I wasn't exempted. I graduated high school at the age of 15 and I was all set to study medicine in college. Unfortunately, I was unable to secure admission into all of the schools I applied to mainly because of Nigeria's corrupt educational system. After spending a year and a half without any positive result, my plans to study abroad became resolute.

Relocating to the United States to study pharmacy was one of the toughest decisions I have made so far. I was only seventeen when I traveled alone to America, leaving my family behind to a destination of the unknown. A few days before leaving Nigeria, I thought the United States was a land of greener pastures - that you don't have to stress yourself to make wealth. Little did I know it was a totally different scenario. Fitting into the culture, different beliefs, and trying to understand how things are done in a different environment were my biggest challenges. There was a time when I was overwhelmed, thinking I was failing all of my classes. I had to meet up with one of my instructors with teary eyes. I explained to him how I could barely understand his accent during lectures and how I might end up failing the class if things continued in that pattern. He was really concerned and encouraged me to have more faith in myself. He said, " I see you are a smart girl, you might think things are tough at the moment but once you are over it, it is done. It only takes extra strength to excel". These words have dwelled in me ever since then; I never allowed negativity to get in my way of success.

Change is constant. People say they never imagined how difficult it might be. The process of adjusting to a new life for me entailed bullying, financial crisis, discrimination, and being intentionally avoided. I grew up speaking English proficiently but coming to this country made me feel less of an English speaker. I was constantly abused and laughed at because of my accent and word choice. I tried to fit in by mimicking the American accent, but this only worsened the case. The worst part of the changes I encountered involved paying for my tuition which I still struggle with to date. As an international student, I am limited to only working on school campuses which can only cover a small percentage of my expenses. I mostly rely on my parents back home and some supportive relations here. They could only do much, so I had to find other ways to survive.

The dollar to Naira exchange became unaffordable for my parents. They couldn't afford to financially sponsor me as they had other responsibilities to take care of. This was a tough time for me; I contemplated going back to my home country because I was on the verge of depression, and it felt like everything around me was failing. I would always have tears on my pillow every night. I had no comfortable shelter. Things became more intense as the days went by. My tuition fees were accumulating; I had no money, nor was there enough food to eat. Things were severely bad for me and I was only eighteen years old. I had seen what life was all about at that age, but I knew going back wasn't an option. I had not come this far to give up now. After a while, I got a full-time job, although not with good pay it was better than none. It was near impossible trying to keep straight A's in my courses with a full course load and a full-time job. But an adage from my tribe says, "Ka sise da a da ki ojo ola wa le dará." In English, it means we should work hard and smart so that our future can be brighter.

Two years after my arrival in the United States, I earned an associate degree in general science. I thought maybe I had been on the wrong path. Growing up in an African-dominated environment, people mostly make you believe that if you are not a doctor, lawyer, nurse, or engineer, you have not made it in life. This was my belief growing up; I wanted to be a medical doctor so that I could make my parents and community proud. But what about making myself proud? What about my passion? Do I really want to be a medical doctor? These are the rhetorical questions I kept asking myself and I had no specific answers to. In order to get answers and find what my passions were, I decided to take a gap year from school. I tried many things, one of which was getting involved in technology. I realized I had more passion for this than any other thing I had tried. I enrolled in an online coding course and I self-taught myself how to code. It was an awesome journey and made me realize that I am capable of doing anything that I believe is outside my reach. After the course was over I returned to school and switched my major to computer science. My parents weren't in support of this, so I tried to make them see my reasons for switching. As expected, they hesitated and tried to tell me back into not switching to an entirely different field, but my mind was already made up.

I am nearly at the end of getting my bachelor's in computer science and I can say I never thought I could make it this far. Although there are still challenges and struggles here and there, no one said it was going to be easy. It is the dream of many students to study abroad, which I think is an interesting prospect. You get to gain a lot of knowledge and broaden your mindset, including getting to learn interesting things about a totally new culture and social setting. Studying abroad could be challenging, but you tend to discover yourself and see things from different perspectives. It also comes with major pros and cons, and I can say I had a fair share of both. But as of right now, I am mostly enjoying the pros

54

and I am grateful things are getting better by the day. I am not where I intend to be but I am getting there. A proverb says, "Rome is not built in a day." I don't expect to miraculously attain success without work and staying focused. Cheers to more success in a foreign land becoming home.

ABISOLA AROWOLAJU (originally from Nigeria) is a current undergraduate student at Morgan State University. Her major and interest lie in the areas of computer science, software engineering, and artificial intelligence. Email: Abisolaarowolaju@gmail.com

17

When I Grow Up, I Want to Be an Oreo

Ife Adedoyin, *Nigeria*

Oreo. Ooooreeeyooo. What exactly is it? Could it be a sandwich cookie? One consisting of two crispy chocolate crusts and a creamy white filling encased inside? Or could it be a disparaging term meant to describe people who have assimilated into "white America"? Specifically, Black people. Specifically, me. The former definition hurled me back into my childhood; it brought about memories of milk mustaches, crumbs beneath my fingernails, and terrible cavities. The latter, quite frankly, left a sour taste in my mouth.

"It's pronounced '*taw-ul*,' not '*to-wel*,' you African booty-scratcher!" I looked at my 3rd-grade childhood bully in confusion. Yet again, I mispronounced a common word. First, it was *three*, now this. I shrunk in embarrassment, not only at my then thick accent but my cultural background as well. I grew to resent my Nigerian roots. The nauseating textile patterns, the stinky food my mom would pack me for lunch, the tight cornrows that left me tender-headed and in pain for days, I wanted nothing to do with it anymore. After that backhanded comment hurled towards me made contact, all I ever wanted was for people to view me as white. I elected to change my mannerisms, my way of dress, the people I conversed with, everything. I even implemented this whitewash of ideas into my home, substituting *egusi soup* and *moin-moin* for the all-American staple, Oreos— much to my parents' dismay. I went the whole nine yards and added a mile. I perceived white as the norm. White was all anyone should aspire to be. White meant that I would not be called an *African booty-scratcher,* whatever that was; I would not be teased for smelling like last night's cooking; I would no longer be the butt of countless African jokes hilarious to everyone but me.

My twisted way of thinking persisted until my sophomore year of high school. Back then, all I ever wanted was to be an *Oreo*—that meant that even though I was black on the outside, my *white* insides would be enough to grab a seat at the table. So even though, in class, my name was a dead giveaway for the background I attempted to mask, my behavior suggested otherwise. My need to belong in white America transcended the traditions and customs my parents strove to instill in me. My resentment for those traditions only increased as I discovered how much easier life was without being outwardly African. After adopting the "American" way of life, I realized it was those same traditions that caused me to stick out like a sore thumb. They made me feel like an outsider, a stranger, someone of no importance. That is, until I saw someone that threw me for a loop. I took notice of some of her features: the facial markings that resembled my grandmother's; the strong accent that mirrored that of my parents; and her thick head of hair that reminded me of me. Past me. Black me. She looked so confident; her face unwavering amidst the sea of white.

I stripped my eyes away from her as some force pulled me into a state of introspection. *Why does she look like that, and... and talk like that?* At that moment, the word *oreo* permeated my mind; it seeped through my pores and caused me to question parts of myself—parts I thought I had changed for the better. I soon realized why her presence disturbed me so much: by whitewashing my identity, I essentially rejected my Nigerian background. The struggles my parents underwent to ensure a better life for our family, the language barrier they overcame when they stepped foot into this country, the determination they upheld to thrive in this new world—I rejected it all. Following my realization, I made a resounding promise to myself. *Never again will I renounce such a vital component of my identity. Never again.*

Fast-forward four years, I am still rediscovering my roots. Back then, all I wanted was to be a walking contradiction—an African on the outside, apparent Caucasian on the inside—so unlearning those habits I placed upon myself is proving difficult. Nonetheless, I am making strides to embrace my Nigerian culture because I refuse to be a stranger in my own home. At the end of the day, am I an Oreo? Presumably. Will I let that define me? Definitely not. I am an Oreo of my own making, one that can belt Big Time Rush's *Boyfriend* on one day and proudly consume *efo* and *eba* on another. I reject the idea that my supposed "white" center symbolizes a renunciation of my background; instead, it is a representation of a newly blank canvas ready to obtain as much color as possible.

IFEOLUWA ADEDOYIN (originally from Nigeria) is an undergraduate student in the School of Computer, Mathematics, and Natural Sciences at Morgan State University, Maryland. Her major research interests lie in clinical, science-based, surgical research. Email: ifade2@morgan.edu

18

American Hunger

Ruth Amara Okolo, *Nigeria*

I came to America with a part of myself that was already whole. Now, I am split in halves, scratching for balance. As a woman coming from a country where women are only accorded respect for the rings on their finger and for their reproductive systems, America gave me a chance to be myself; single, living for my dreams and aspirations: carving my boats and tossing them into the river of opportunities. Seeing it move. But what America did not tell me was what it would do to my mental health.

Immigrant, Little Grant
America makes you confident. From the moment I stepped off the plane in 2019 for my master's program. I felt like I could conquer the world. My world, that is, the one I had lived in my country Nigeria, stifled with nepotism, unhappiness, and slow achievements. That world crumbled to dust at the border when I presented my student visa, and it was stamped with an entry approval. I felt a heaviness drop from me, the belief that I would never be able to further my studies beyond the undergraduate. I came into being in 2010. Light took over. The door opened for me. I felt so triumphant, I smiled at the border official. And even though he did not smile back, I felt nothing but trickles of joy and a filling relief. For a person coming of no privilege of place, power or wealth, this was the greatest milestone I had achieved in my life. It was not publishing three books at age twenty-four, not becoming a lawyer at age twenty-five. Of all my life achievements, it was coming to America as an immigrant. It was the greatest of all.

A Story with no Words
How else can you tell a story without verbal iterations? For me, it has always been art--painting and drawing. One time, it became photography. The first time I visited the United States, I was lucky to have been selected as a writing resident of the University of Iowa. This special four-months residency gave me the chance to visit six cities in the county: from New York to Chicago, New Orleans to Iowa, Pittsburgh to Washington DC. It gave me the chance to see the world I had only visualized through the colored TV screen of my family home in Nigeria. It made me believe it was real. I ate the famous deep-dish pizza in Chicago, danced through the French Quarter with a procession band, green beads in one hand and a grenade drink in the other. I cried sitting beside the

plaque stones with the names of the enslaved at the Whitney Plantation. I stood in Time Square at nighttime, enthralled by the digital visions of Manhattan. From the steps of the Lincoln Memorial, I watched the capitol grace the horizon in its glory. And until the days of my trip ended, I believed more and more in this country I want to call home.

Hunger

My hunger for placement began as I became older. Oh, how beautiful it must be to call somewhere home as easily as an American. I noticed this difference between me and this new world I settled more in but felt more out. People say to me "let's go hiking," and I wonder why. Why venture into the woods, where silence and the animals who call it home reside? Why not stay here, where you have much knowledge, more vicinity and recognized terrain? Then I realized it was what being American meant. adventure. The hunger for it. You can go wherever you want to go without thinking about it. For me, it is a luxury of privilege I am startled with, still. One I may never get in this lifetime.

The joys of being here outweigh the unpleasantness. I learnt how to drive here, how to make an espresso and Americano while working as a barista. I learnt how to ski, to go on walks with no aim of destination but just to look at the world and all her beauty. My education as a graduate student brought me so much knowledge, community, and versatile intelligence that I did not have back in my country. I have seen how big the world is and how small I am in it. And vice versa.

There have also been pains. The constant dread of no definite placement, no place I can call home. I feel so much at home here, but is it, really? No. As an international student, I know my limitations outweigh the feeling of home here no matter how much it seeks to creep in, to establish itself within my spirits. But if there is anything America has allowed me to do it is to live all my lives. All the women in me; Nigerian, African, Black, all of them are alive here. And that, each day, makes me grateful.

RUTH OKOLO is a graduate student in the School of English at Morgan State University. Her major research interests center on the area of creative writing, academic literacies, women and gender, academic integrity, and multicultural research. Email: ruoko@morgan.edu

19

International Student Experience: Land of the Free

Omolade Ola, *Nigeria*

I left Nigeria (the only country I ever knew) for the United States at 17. I remember being excited as I packed my bags to get ready for the next phase of my life. I kept thinking to myself, this is an end to my daily errand runs; an end to my mum still thinking I am a child, and an end to sharing a room with my younger sister. I was now an adult! Or so I thought. As the car pulled out of the compound, streams of tears flowed down my cheeks amidst the smiling. It took me a while to figure out why I was crying uncontrollably. Soon, I realized I was moving away from my mum and sister, the two people that mattered the most to me. My mum noticed me crying, and she too started crying amidst telling me this was a thing of joy; I was fulfilling the American dream. The American dream had been sold to me from a very young age of 9 when my favorite aunt left the country pursuing better education. Back in Nigeria, America is seen as a country that changes the status of every man whose foot touches the ground. I expected that as soon as I arrived, my dream to build houses for my mum would be actualized, as money sprouted on trees.

I soon realized that all my imaginations and fantasies of meeting Justin Bieber at the airport and falling in love or meeting Barack Obama and being awarded a scholarship were beautiful fantasies. I came out of the BWI airport in Baltimore to meet my aunt's friend, who was waiting to pick me up, and I sighed deeply. "America is just a country," I thought. This thought soon faded by the thrill of me seeing how beautiful the roads were. Although it was around 9 p.m., I could see how well-lit the city was with beautiful buildings that trailed the path of each side of the road.

Arriving on campus the first day of class, August 24th, 2015, I hurriedly made my way to class as early as 7:30 am. I was the first to arrive as class was not starting till 9 am. Usually, I would use this early start to find something to read or nap. However, the thrill of finally being a college student was so real that kept giggling at various thoughts that crossed my mind. Soon, students started to troop in, and I wished to feel included. I kept looking at the features of every brown-skinned person that came in to assess if they had "Nigerian" features. Tomike walked into class, and I instantly felt more comfortable because I could tell she was Nigerian as well. Though her accent sounded very British, more fluent than the average Nigerian- British accent, I could tell she was Yoruba. I could not wait for class to be over to make my first friendship. I introduced myself to her after class and soon found out she also just relocated from Nigeria. I instantly knew I had no reason to feel inferior as I was not alone.

I soon found myself in the company of five other Nigerians who were also studying electrical engineering and shared a similar background. We spent many nights studying together, working on various projects, comparing grades, and striving for better one, applying to internships and research opportunities. I received many rejections while searching for the right summer internship. Due to the laws that govern international students, companies were not opened to employing F-1 holders as we are often called. Because of this, none of us obtained any internship opportunities despite our high GPAs. We stopped attending career conferences and career fairs as we saw no point in it. I always said, if one of us had gotten an opportunity, we would all have had a reason to keep trying. However, looking back, I see how fixated on applying to the companies we knew of, we failed to see other companies that saw value in giving international students a chance.

I often heard the phrase, "You will be done before you know it" from older friends and strangers alike when they asked me what year I was in, even as a freshman. I remember rolling my eyes every time thinking, "so they say". But before I realized it, four years was almost up, and I was about to graduate. I knew I wanted my mum at my graduation. I couldn't wait to walk across the stage with my mum cheering me from her seat, so I had to make sure all her documents to take to the embassy had to be ready. I kept bugging my mum from my first semester senior year to renew her international passport but being a typical Nigerian mum, she didn't see the need for the fuss. She said, "We still have time, don't worry." She started her passport processing renewal in February of 2019, 3 months before my graduation. This should be enough time to get her passport and go for her visa appointment. However, we discovered the passport offices were almost out of paper, so there was a long waitlist of people. So, what would have taken about 2 weeks to obtain ended up taking two months. With so much hope, I still went ahead to try getting her a visa appointment date, but it wasn't until a week before my graduation I had to be ok with the fact that my mum would miss my graduation. It hurt more than I ever thought it would, but I knew the fact that her daughter was becoming a bachelor's degree holder was enough for her. Hence, I mentally prepared myself for the rest of my future to be ok with her not always being at every milestone in my life. Though I knew the longing for her would always linger.

Overall, relocating to America, I have learned the value of culture. I despised being a Nigerian growing up. I cannot put my finger on it when that feeling started, but I remember telling my classmates in secondary school (middle and high school) that I was not Nigerian. In my heart, I was not lying as I did not feel I resonated with being Nigerian. I didn't even see the value of my native dialect, Yoruba, that I introduce myself as Diana, which is my middle name as opposed to Omolade, my first name. I had to travel 5,395 miles from Lagos,

Nigeria, to Baltimore, Maryland, to love and appreciate my culture. The beauty of being able to talk on the phone with my mum in a public space without people preying, or being able to enjoy other cultures, or simply enjoying a nice bowl of scorching wings on the cold winter night. I had to learn to set goals for myself and accomplish them because my life and future depended on them. I no longer lived life simply because of what my mum would say but because it would move me closer to my life goals. Though my friends and family often laugh and say I am now "Westernized" in my thinking, I believe this experience has made me have a full and robust view of life.

References

Clark, N. (2009, September 1). *What defines an international student? A look behind the numbers.* Retrieved from World Education News + Reviews: https://wenr.wes.org/2009/09/wenr-september-2009-feature

Skinner, K. G. (2020, January 27th). *International Students.* Retrieved from Encyclopedia: https://www.encyclopedia.com/education/encyclopedias-almanacs-transcripts-and-maps/

OMOLADE OLA (originally from Nigeria), is a graduate student in the School of Computer science, studying Data Science in Advanced Computing. Her major research interests are machine learning, and data science applications. Email: omola5@morgan.com

20

My Experience as an International Student during the COVID Pandemic

Tolulope Ajayi, *Nigeria*

Towards the end of 2019, I got news of the existence of COVID-19 in China, and it sounded dreadful because it was an unknown and dangerous virus with no known cure. I began to hope that it would remain in China and not spread to other parts of the world. However, by early 2020, it was in many countries of the world, but I hoped it would rescind. The most dreaded thing for me was the rate the pandemic was taking lives. At this point, borders were closed, and I could not travel to my country to be with my family. All I could do was pray. Many institutions in the United States, including Morgan State University, began to announce the transitioning of classes to online studies, and the offices started working from home. All activities came to an abrupt halt, and it was as if the world was coming to an end. Going to stores for provision was a dilemma for fear of being infected and to make matters worse, all news on TV was on COVID-19 and the death toll kept increasing at an alarming rate. The news media did not help the situation. The news communicated that the virus was capable of leading many to their death–it was very depressing and could make fragile minds hypertensive. It got so bad that I had to stop watching the news on COVID. I also advised many people against constantly listening to the news because of what was being sent out.

As if this was not enough, my contract as an intern ended and was not renewed because the governor of the state of Maryland placed a hold on all forms of employment. My employer tried to renew my contract all to no avail and as a result, I became jobless. This was the first time I became be jobless since I came to study in the US. As a student, I have always been lucky to have a place to work as an intern with a renewed contract yearly. It was a very hard transition because I never planned on being jobless and I had many bills to pay. I searched for jobs on campus for several months but did not get any. At this time, Morgan State University supported several international students financially because most of these students lost their jobs at the onset of the pandemic. This was well applauded and appreciated by the international students.

Morgan State University was supportive during the period of the pandemic. They made the transition to online classes easy. The university already has a mechanism for online classes in place, this made it easy for me to understand the processes for online classes. They also communicated with the students regularly on information about the COVID 19 pandemic and other issues. The lecturers were also very understanding during this period, and they were ready to support as many students as necessary. Morgan State University also set up a support program for international students through the office of the Vice President of International Affairs. This was unexpected and impressive; they were able to help with the guidelines and information necessary for traveling despite the closed borders. This initiative was a relief to many international students, although the program was not able to help with the most daunting issue which was getting a job to help cope with the financial situation.

Despite the adverse effects of COVID-19, I discovered that the pandemic brought a lot of positive transitions with it. Technology became more advanced to make room for communication during this period. Technologically adverse individuals were forced to learn how to use several platforms for meetings, graduations, and other programs. Also, students and professors that commute over a long distance to get to school now have the option of an online or hybrid class.

Irrefutably, the period of COVID-19 is one that people will not forget in a hurry. Many people lost their loved ones and others got separated from their families for a while. As an international student at MSU, the pandemic has added to my experiences. I have also been motivated to be more proactive and far-sighted in my decisions.

TOLULOPE AJAYI (originally from Nigeria) is a graduate student in the School of Education and Urban Studies. Her major research includes international students' success, student retention, and higher education research. Email: toaja2@morgan.edu

21

My Cross-Cultural Study Experience: An American Dream Achieved

Fatima K. Babih, *Sierra Leone*

I am from Sierra Leone, West Africa where most women are either illiterate or semi-literate at best. My academic journey reflects a struggle to disrupt this reality faced by millions of women in my country and similar societies. I developed a love and aptitude for learning at an early age and was encouraged by my mother's fight to keep me in school, against my father's will. My mother, who was illiterate, would urge me to keep up with my studies because, according to her, a beautiful woman must also be educated to achieve progress in society. My father was an Islamic scholar who also encouraged me to learn, but he did not want me to attain a western education; instead, he emphasized studying our Islamic religious text, the Holy Quran. In fact, he forbade me from helping my mother in the kitchen because he thought it would take me away from studying. Thus, both my parents, in their own ways, influenced my passion and drive to get on a lifelong education journey. Unfortunately, Sierra Leone society places higher value on marriage for girls than schooling; most girls in our country never finish secondary school because they get married early. Consequently, my pursuit of education was hindered by compulsory arranged marriage when I was only 15 years old.

The Beginning of a Lifelong Journey
Before I left Sierra Leone, however, I sought alternative ways to continue my education, and since I did not complete secondary school, my only option in Sierra Leone was vocational training. So, I attended the Opportunities Industrialization Center (OIC), a vocational institute founded by an African American Baptist Minister, Reverend Leon Sullivan. Attending OIC provided me with respite for my frustrated pursuit of education. While I was excited to be in a learning environment again, especially learning to type and do basic bookkeeping, two years at OIC did not provide me with the literacy I needed. When I later arrived in America, I was a semi-literate young woman with a thirst for education. I learned that in America, it was possible for a school dropout like me to attain education. Knowing there were opportunities to continue learning rekindled my hope and formed my American dream of attaining higher education.

My American Dream

My cross-cultural story about studying in America began in New York City with GED classes by mail (pre-internet era), then night classes at a local high school and community college. I was excited to explore every available opportunity. Once I earned my GED, doors opened for me to pursue a college degree. I was accepted at City University of New York, Baruch College then transferred to Queens College (QC), which is a more traditional university setting. The diverse student body at QC helped me feel a sense of belonging on an academic campus. Furthermore, at QC I gained academic endurance and success through Search for Education, Elevation, and Knowledge (SEEK), a program designed for academically disadvantaged students. As a student in SEEK, I benefited from intensive workshops, and a well-structured support network and learning communities. SEEK also provided tutoring in math, English and other subjects, as well as guidance counseling, financial aid, and campus daycare for my two young children. Even with all the support from SEEK, I struggled to work, care for my children and study. I eventually earned my bachelor's degree in economics from QC and this achievement strengthened my confidence and resolve to further my education. However, despite continued nurturing of my American dream, my personal hardships, including divorce and single motherhood, forced me to put my pursuit of higher education on hold, which lasted over 20 years.

A Lifelong Journey Resumed

I made the difficult decision to resume my American dream of pursuing higher education while in my 50s, when my children were more independent. I enrolled at Towson University where I earned a master's degree in Gender Studies. But my thirst for higher education was still unquenched, leading to my pursuit of another masters' degree in Legal Studies at the University of Baltimore (UB). My experience at UB was like that at Queens College; I felt nurtured and supported by my department and professors in many ways. I thrived at UB and even participated in study abroad in Tanzania where I completed a course in human rights and capacity building. Graduating from UB with a 3.7 GPA strengthened my confidence to strive for the highest level of education. My American dream was realized when I was accepted at Morgan State University (MSU). Achieving my American dream at an HBCU was a crowning success for my educational journey. I could not wish for a better academic experience. The Community College Leadership Doctoral Program at MSU has reinforced my confidence in my career choice and lifelong purpose of helping students achieve academic success. Looking back on my journey, I appreciate that each institution I attended, along with its people, contributed positively to my ultimate success. This realization influences my passion, as an emerging community college leader, to pay it forward by becoming an effective advocate and leader in helping students achieve their dreams of attaining higher education and workforce preparedness, regardless of where their journeys begin. My passion is well aligned

 with my career aspirations in the community college system, a system dedicated to promoting access and equity in higher education. I believe that my journey represents the stories of women from disadvantaged backgrounds who, through resilience and determination, achieve their dreams of higher education attainment. And it is also a story that I hope will demonstrate how alternative education pathways and supportive academic environments can propel students, even those from disadvantaged backgrounds, to achieve academic success and self-determination.

(In the picture: Towson graduation with my two older children who attended QC Day Care when my journey started)

FATIMA BABIH (originally from Sierra Leone) earned a doctoral degree in Community College Leadership Doctoral Program in the School of Education and Urban Studies. Her major research interests include higher education leadership and policy, community college student affairs, women, and gender policies. Email: fawah1@morgan.edu

22

Postgraduate Studies: A Lifelong Experience on Teaching and Learning

Shuaibu Hassan Usman, *Nigeria*

As a son to a father whose occupation is nomadic – cattle rearing in the remote area of Barkin Ladi, Plateau state, Nigeria– I experienced a lot of life changing situations. It all started when my father decided to educate himself and his children on western education (*Boko in Hausa language*) in early 1970s. His decision resulted in enrolling his ten children, both males and females, in western school system with seven of them having higher education qualifications. I am among his children that acquired a university degree, which resulted in being offered a graduate assistant at the university. During my days as a student in high school and university, I was used to assisting my family with nomadic activities during holidays. However, as an employee of a university, I didn't have much time to assist them anymore. In the course of my work, I started acquiring experience in teaching and learning such as assessment, examinations' conduct and setting, students' counseling, advising, and student-staff relationship.

My lifelong experience of teaching and learning have increased greatly when I enrolled into postgraduate studies in Malaysia and United States of America. In Malaysia, I enrolled into a master's degree program at the International Islamic University Malaysia (IIUM) in 2012 and completed it by May 2014. As an international student in Malaysia and an academic fellow in Nigeria, I gained a lot of experience in teaching and learning methods and culture of patience. The experiences gained on teaching and learning methods include learning about the goal of education, which is not only getting excellent grades but also enhanced academic performance such as knowledge retention, social interaction, and academic sincerity. In my entire school life, I have not experienced an open examination usually called take-home exam until after my enrollment as a master student in Malaysia. I learned how teamwork contributes to students' academic performance and I found it invaluable in my postmaster degree teaching methods. Another aspect that captured my mind was the way IIUM discourages a single type of assessment method in that assessments were broken down into many components such as group project, homework, term paper, midterm exam, and final exam. The final exam is allocated with a maximum of 30 percent, although the course lecture has the discretion to modify it. In Nigeria, the

68

grading system is that 30 percent is allocated for continues assessment (CA) while 70 percent for final examination. The 70 % of the final exam is to be taken only once without any second attempt. Afterwards, the final grade of students is determined by the CA and exam only. The experience I gained on culture of patience is that everyone obeys queues and patient enough to listen to conversations before acting. For example, we used to have 15 minutes break in a 3-hour lecture to go to canteen, and on many occasions, I have seen our professors queuing behind us to get their order without showing *big-time* (difference). No wonder, Frank Abate who is a Division Manager at JM&A Group has to say "The beauty of studying abroad is gaining a broader understanding of other cultures. Having access to other people and building relationships with those people on their home turf enables one to think more creatively and flexibly, necessary skills in today's competitive work environment. If a student can bring that understanding and knowledge back to the USA, the sky's the limit!" (The Institute of International Education, 2021).

My second journey in postgraduate studies is the doctoral degree at the Morgan State University, Baltimore, MD, United States of America. This is my second year in the PhD program; however, I gained experience on teaching philosophy, teaching online class, research-based evidence, teaching portfolio, and a culture of accommodating students with learning disabilities and lifestyles. The experience I gained in teaching philosophy is that the classroom must be safe and conducive for learning in terms of freedom of expression. Additionally, I learned that teaching philosophy is about training, practice, and experience you offer to learners. In teaching philosophy, I learned every student has a unique and special talent to offer in education, hence, you need to create an environment for them to learn through incorporating oral, written, and visual components in the course content and understand their differences in terms of culture, gender, race, sexual orientation, different levels of ability, otherness, and social background as well as encourage them to explore their capabilities and accept themselves for who they are. In my previous teaching and learning experience, I have never imagined or experienced the need for teaching philosophy. What I know back home is that department allocates courses and their contents, which the lecturers build their teaching notes on and deliver to students. Now I am seeing the differences in learning environment between my country and the United States.

I learned how to teach an online class. As a doctoral student in school of Management, I had to enroll into teaching practicum class in your second year to teach undergraduate courses. As the pandemic of COVID 19 hit the United States and the world, Morgan State University adopted flex mode of teaching in which some students will be in class (in-person) and others will be online (virtual). We were taught how to create and handle the flex mode of teaching, which gives me a lifelong experience on teaching online class.

On the side of research-based evidence, I learned how to create and assess research-based evidence through defining and identifying the PICOC

(Population, Intervention, Comparison, Outcome/Objective, and Context), developing a search strategy, creating an inclusion criterion, and assigning critical appraisal of the methodological quality aspect, sample size, method of analysis, and measurement scales. This research-based evidence has given me a unique experience on conducting and writing research.

In teaching portfolio, I learned how to create and use rubrics for assessment as well as developing a rich lesson plan that contains learning outcomes, course objectives, learning activities, statement of teaching philosophy, grading policy, learning plans, syllabus, and detail course schedule. This is my first time of learning how to create teaching portfolio.

I learned that teaching is about a culture of accommodating students with learning disabilities and lifestyles by being an open and inclusive to all students who have obstacles in achieving their full potential through creating flexibility to work with students who have some learning difficulties or disabilities. Similarly, I learned to consider students' lifestyles in learning environment such as sexual orientation and appearance. In our society back home, it is a taboo to permit alternate kind of lifestyles.

My postgraduate studies have taught me not only teaching and learning but also the culture of openness, great job opportunities, policies that work, infrastructures for the people, freedom, simplifying life using technology and how to manage challenges in fitting into American lifestyle and living.

Hassan U. Shuaibu (originally from Nigeria) is a doctoral student in Information Science and System in the School of Business, Morgan State University. His major research interests lie in the areas of big data analytics, knowledge management, information system, and information technology governance. Email: hashu1@morgan.edu. Email: hasusman@gmail.com

23

Long Way to the United States

Ramina Javid, *Iran*

Usually, it takes around 15 hours to fly from my country, Iran, to the United States. So, when people ask me how many hours it takes; the expected answer is 15 hours. Surprisingly, in my case, the answer is 15 days! You might probably wonder why something like this would happen? The answer is COVID-19!

I started applying to universities to pursue my Ph.D. in 2020, and before I knew it, the COVID-19 pandemic happened. Everything was unexpected, and it was unclear when the situation would return to normal. Imagine emailing professors and saying I want to pursue my Ph.D. in another country while you do not know when you will get out of quarantine! Despite all of this, I was accepted to a Ph.D. program. I thought that the hard part was over, but that was just the beginning! Because of the pandemic, all government institutions, including embassies, were closed. It took me seven months to book an appointment to get my visa. As you might guess, getting the visa was not the hard part either.

At the time of my trip, my country was experiencing its third wave of the COVID-19, and I had to quarantine myself in another country for 14 days to enter the United States. But here I am, against all odds, after 5 polymerase chain reaction (PCR) and COVID-19 tests and 15 days quarantine, writing this essay from my apartment in Baltimore, exactly one year after these events!

My experience of studying abroad is different from what I have heard before from other students. I arrived in the United States right before the new year, and since the beginning, it was hard for me to settle in. For the first semester, I did not meet any of my classmates or professors in person! It didn't feel real since everything was online. Online classes were fun at first because you can comfortably sit behind your desk, drink your coffee, and listen to a lecture about sustainability in transportation. But after a while, I felt kind of isolated. Teamwork did not have the expected result, and it was not satisfying. It wasn't easy to work with people I had never met in person. I also missed the time in classes and talking to other students outside of the classrooms.

After the vaccines were developed, slowly everything returned to normal, and I managed to go to university for the first time. Some classes are still online, but the joy of talking to students and faculty face to face is invaluable. If we ignore wearing masks and using hand sanitizers constantly (just for opening a door!), everything is perfect as I imagined it would be. I hope that everything will return to normal soon.

For several years, my goal has been to study and get my Ph.D. in the United States, and when the pandemic started, I thought it would never happen. We all learned a lot during this difficult time. But the most important lesson for me was to never stop chasing your dreams, even if you are facing a global pandemic!

RAMINA JAVID (originally from Iran) is a Ph.D. student in the Transportation & Urban Infrastructure Studies Program in the School of Engineering. Her major research interests include equity in transportation, travel behavior, safety, and big data analysis. Email: rajah1@morgan.edu

24

Fortitude and Perseverance in the Face of Discomfort, Discouragement, and Challenge

Antonia Nwogbo, *Nigeria*

A 6th-century Greek philosopher named Pythagoras left an indelible mark in my mind during my secondary/high school days. He influenced my commitment to education; I was motivated to develop great enthusiasm for mathematics and went on to college to study statistics and mathematics because of the Pythagoras Theorem and similar works. My goal was to earn a doctorate; use my knowledge to research and contribute to mankind. I worked to support myself and my education during my undergraduate schooling as there was no financial aid or loans. This new enlightenment motivated me to pursue my education with great ambition. Against various obstacles such as limited financial support, I knew that my experience coming from Nigeria prepared me for what it would take to succeed as an international student in America.

As an international student from Nigeria, I came to America two years after graduating college with the equivalent of a BS in statistics and math and to further my education. The goal was to pursue graduate studies in statistics and continue my aspiration of earning a mathematics doctoral degree that would enable advancement in knowledge and skills to facilitate discovery for the contribution and betterment of mankind. Upon arrival, there were many socio-political dilemmas that most international students face when studying abroad. These issues consist of a residency visa, employment, obtaining transcripts, tuition, and fees, and healthcare, among others. One of the hardships I recall most vividly in my transition to America was my time working for a company called Kirby. I went door to door selling Kirby vacuum cleaner (ostentatiously called a sales job). This is nothing other than cleaning house for those people who would allow you to come into their homes, so they take advantage of free vacuuming of their home, clean their curtains, and other chores to demonstrate the efficiency of Kirby with the goal they buy it. I used the word *ostentatious* twofold—one because it is the job title used in the advertisement to get you to apply/get sucked into employment without benefits/pay unless you make sales and get a commission. Two, a saying in my culture is "O ke afa ne gbu nwan nkita" i.e., *"Big-name-that-kills-a-small-dog"*. As it turned out, that is exactly what that job was, and after two weeks of laborious paid-for-nothing-wasted-time, I quit the job without a dime. Another odd job was working at a dry cleaner under the horrid heat of steaming and ironing clothes; these were hard/difficult times.

I missed my home country, my family, friends, and my great job (executive sales representative) at a great and prestigious computer company (that sent us on training outside the country to places like London, Zimbabwe, Ethiopia, and Barcelona). Finally, I got a job as a teller in a US Bank, Oregon. I was *over the moon* for a prestigious job in a bank with benefits/and perks, such as tuition reimbursement. I worked for six months and one day was told to leave without explanation; it was their prerogative to terminate my employment as it was mine at any time without questions asked. My performance/work ethic was excellent; customers loved my professionalism, courteousness, friendliness, and respectfulness, the detailed attention to their needs; always greeting customers by their names, they loved my accent. It was one of the reasons I was hired, to add diversity to the staff and such a lovely accent with British English. I was devastated, for I believed and had been told and praised for my efficiency and detailed orientation in handling transactions. I soon learned that the very attributes that got me hired would be the cause of my termination when they were no longer useful to the company. It was annihilating, I felt like the world was on its axes. I had hoped to advance my career as a banker and continue my education. All I had worked for seemed to be in vain, vanquished with a single word—*dismissed*, employment terminated, but as we say in my culture, "Chukwu na sh ulu efi ne wen ro odudu igigi": *"God drives away the flies for a cow without a tail."*

During my time working in the bank, I had been making the acquaintance of a fellow indigene through phone connection, the brother to a college friend back home. We had met before I left for America and exchanged phone numbers. He came to visit home, Nigeria after 4 years, after completing his undergraduate studies. We got married 20 months after my arrival in the US and I moved to Charlotte, NC to start another phase in life. I was able to obtain permanent residency and ten years later we both became citizens of America, Yeh!

We both had goals to pursue our graduate studies and start a family after three years. We were blessed with a child within our first month of marriage and I gave birth to a sweet, lovely baby boy a month before our first wedding anniversary. As God would have it, I got a job at the bank again before my pregnancy was evident as it provided the needed health insurance and benefits for my family. We deferred our goals for graduate studies for later, but I encouraged my husband to consider part-time schooling while I concentrate on the family for now. Our second baby girl was born three years later, and six years later, our third child. I wanted to be the best in whatever I applied myself to, so

I deferred personal educational goals for the near future while I focused on my role as a mother.

I changed my career after the birth of my third child and went into education. My career change was brought about by a combination of several factors—my need to contribute to mankind in whatever way possible, thus the volunteering in my children's school, my love for children, for the power of education, and for mathematics. Through volunteer work with little ones in elementary and middle school, I experienced the joy of making a difference in the lives of my little friends, observing the changes/growth, and their accomplishments in both academics and emotional/social skills in self-efficacy. An epiphany in my career path ensued, I figured, what better way to do what I love most, teaching math. I decided to become a teacher and pursue Master's of Arts in Teaching (MAT) at University of Maryland Baltimore County, part-time. However, I changed my route of completing the MAT program due to financial constraints and timely completion.

After I became a certified teacher, it did not make sense to continue with the MAT program, so I enrolled with McDaniel College for Curriculum and Instruction with a concentration in Leadership as a cohort member. I left the school system where the cohort was established. I could not continue the program and accepted life as it was. I began to feel unfulfilled and disconcerted, unable to discern why. I am blessed with a beautiful family, lovely children, a loving and caring husband, a career as a teacher, so why this melancholy? Upon deep reflection and closer look at my life, I realized I had fulfilled almost all my goals, except obtaining a doctoral degree! I had given up on this aspiration due to a life-threatening illness that involved brain surgery a year after the birth of my third child. But after my soul searching, I knew, I had to at least try to get a graduate degree to help alleviate my discomfiture.

I chose to pursue special education because I believe the skills and knowledge gained will be most beneficial in teaching all learners while I strive to work towards my goals of providing learners with mathematical experiences that I as a student experienced long ago with the work of Greek Philosopher, Pythagoras. Once I completed my MS in Special Education, my longtime aspiration to earn a doctoral degree was resurrected and made feasible. I challenged myself to begin my doctoral journey at age fifty.

At last, I am living the fulfillment of my educational aspiration. I teach high school math where, as always, I worked in culturally diversified schools. It can be a challenge to motivate students to want to learn and be successful, but by advancing my knowledge and teaching methods, I hope to be a better and highly qualified educator, becoming more capable of dealing with different facets of the problems and barriers that confront our children in their pursuit of education. These problems present a great challenge to educators, as they try to teach students that would have been more receptive to academic instructions under normal circumstances. Thus, I redirected my aspirational goals to mathematics education and after an extensive search and comparisons for colleges that offer this course, Morgan State University offered the best program and costs for my needs.

The program is aimed at practitioners who view critical inquiry as a major part of teachers' work and responds to the need of "highly qualified" teachers who want to "develop sensitivity to the characteristics and needs of urban students in general, and African-American students in particular, including the peculiarities of urban environment and institutions, and the implications in teaching and learning of mathematics in such settings, to effect positive changes in the teaching and learning of mathematics at all levels of educational systems" (Morgan State University, 2013, pp. 1). It very much resonates with my goals to effect positive changes in teaching and learning, as testified in my dissertation research interest—The Cognitive Effects of Trauma and Its Impact on African American Students' Mathematics Performance. My educational goal pursuit has been a long and arduous journey, but with fortitude and focus, I am almost at the end of it with the hope of realizing my aspiration!

Morgan State University, *Math Education Program (EdD)*
https://www2.morgan.edu/aslp/edd-mathed

ANTONIA NWOGBO (originally from Nigeria) is a doctoral student in the Mathematics Education Program in the School of Education and Urban Studies. Her major research interests include teaching and learning in mathematics, instructional leadership, and educational policy. Email: annwo3@morgan.edu

25

Colour, Color, Me

Martha Kakooza, *Uganda*

Starting to write, the thought of writing, and the process of writing were things that I became quite familiar being a Women and Gender Studies major. However, writing has often been an anxiety ridden process for me. Fear is often tied to that anxiety. I was filled with fear that I would not fulfill the given page numbers and word count assigned. My fear is most intense at the discovery of the weight of my own voice which in this essay I will correlate with my identity. I will be defining the term identity as the way in which I am understood academically based on my gender, race, nationality, and immigration status. Given that I have been a student most of my life, academia has played a major role in the ways in which I reflect on my identity. In this essay, I will be discussing how I am building critical consciousness regarding the role of my social identities as they are represented in my academic writing journey in the US.

I was placed in an English Speakers of Other Languages class in my first semester of my freshman year because I was a foreign national despite coming from an English-speaking background. Often students can test out of these courses, but I was not given that option. For our class assignments, Dr. Lisa required us to turn in hard copies and called us to her office to give us feedback on our papers.

One fateful Wednesday evening, it was my turn to go into her office. I was feeling so confident about my paper that right before going into her office, I, with an ice-cream cone in hand, was chatting with a friend. I ran up five flights of stairs and sat confidently in the chair across from hers. She started, "When you first walked into my class, hearing you speak and the discussions we have around the book, I thought you were too advanced to be in my course." She paused, and I half-smiled because I noticed her use of past tense in the statement she made. I thought to myself, "she thought? She thought?" She continued, "I am glad I didn't write the transfer over because you are struggling with your spelling." She handed my paper back to me with red marks all over it. A few words stood out to me: "programme," "colour," and "neighbours." I sank into the chair as I felt a hot tear drop onto my paper. "What was going on?" She proceeded to turn to her computer screen. "Your analysis was great. You are doing well with Modern Language Association citations; however, in American English, your spelling was amiss. I will give you full credit for the assignment if you do it over." I did not have time to explain myself, nor did I want to because I felt a lump form up in my throat. I sniffled and said, "Thank you, I will have a quick turnaround" as I rushed to the restroom to get myself together before class which started at 5pm. I thought to myself "how can a college professor with the

77

running claim of working with international students be so heartless? Surely it is a known fact that most international students that have a background in English learned British English."

This was one of the first times I had put myself out there in my writing. As Dr. Lisa spoke, all I could hear was that I was better off reciting multiplication tables. I felt rejected as a writer. My anxiety towards writing assignments increased, I had been misunderstood and undervalued as an immigrant in the United States. I came to learn that this was going to be a huge part of my identity living here.

Finding my voice through the stories of others: Race and nationality

I was in my second year as a Women and Gender Studies major. At this point in my academic writing journey, I had the opportunity to read and cite the works of Gloria Anzaldúa, bell hooks, among others, who wrote with such courage. They took ownership of who they were and, in some cases, used their vernacular English in academically acclaimed work. However, I still did not identify with the writings of these women as an African immigrant. I took up the challenge the summer before junior year to read the works of different female African authors, and especially liked the writings of Chimamanda Adiche Ngozi. She wrote about the nuanced stories of Africans grappling with their Blackness as their salient social identity in America in her novel *Americanah* (2013). This was a part of my social identity that I had begun to explore with constant discussions around race in my coursework. Reading *Americanah* gave me a better understanding of what it meant to be a Black immigrant in the United States. Adichie (2013) wrote about how on many occasions race-ethnicity would be more salient than gender. She emphasized that sometimes as an immigrant you would have to compromise some aspects of your native culture to embrace a new one (2013). *Americanah* not only gave words to my experiences but gave me hope for an adjusted life as well.

After the long summer of reading Adiche's work and falling in love with my Blackness, I had to submit a term paper in Dr. Rio's Feminist Economies course during the Fall semester of my junior year. Dr. Rio gave us the option to explore a topic whose relevance matters to us. The only requirement of the term paper was that it had to explore the lived experience of a person in Baltimore participating in a feminist economy. Feminist economies for Dr. Rio's course were defined as employment opportunities that did not generate profit for sole use within the realms of a capitalist economy. This could include stay at home mothers, social entrepreneurs, worker cooperatives, among others. I decided to tell the story of Gabi, a micro-social entrepreneur and Ghanaian immigrant in Baltimore who started an African cuisine business. In line with social entrepreneurship, the proceeds of Gabi's business went to teaching African college students at UMBC how to cook their traditional African meals in thirty minutes or less. Gabi's life closely mirrored the ones I had read about in

Americanah (Adichie, 2013). Because of the fast-paced nature of American society, she had adjusted and learned how to cook Ghanaian dishes in thirty minutes. In contrast with more traditional Ghanaian dishes that take at least an hour for a bowl of soup. This assignment facilitated a deeper understanding of my race-ethnicity as a social identity as I chose to write about an individual whose social identities closely matched mine.

The week after submitting the paper, Dr. Rio called me into her office. When responding to her email, I had flashbacks of my time in freshman year in Dr. Lisa's office. I walked into Dr. Rio's office, and she had a huge smile on her face. Dr. Rio never smiled; she was on the more stoic side. I sat in the chair across from hers, and she congratulated me for writing the best paper she had seen in a while. This unexpected praise academically was an affirming factor in my developing identity as a Black female international student in the United States.

Conclusion

A geyser of anxiety often erupts deep inside me, spurting fear whenever I think of my academic writing journey. I grew up with my dreams already dreamt for me. There was my loving father, whose hopes were that medical school would secure a better future for me and that a life in America would open doors that were never opened for him. My instructors thought I would be better off not improving my writing because I could recite a few multiplication tables. I had to divorce dreams that were not mine, and work to discover my social identities while trying to be a scholar of these very social identities. I have found that I am on a journey with my writing that is closely linked to my understanding and affirming of my identity. This journey is not a static event, but an excursion that requires continual exploration of self.

Adichie, C. N. (2013). *Americanah*. Anchor.

--

MARTHA KAKOOZA is a graduate student in the School of Higher Education at Morgan State University. Her major research interests include African immigration, STEM education research, higher education, gender, and Black transnationalism. Email: makak1@morgan.edu

26

From Kenya to the US: My Experience of Completing a Master's Degree at an HBCU

Collins Oswago, *Kenya*

I was born and raised in Kenya and did my undergraduate degree in gender and development studies at Egerton University. While growing up, the idea of studying in the United States of America was always a fantasy that seemed hard to achieve. I have always admired the American culture, the education system, and the quality of their degree programs with America having some of the best rated universities worldwide. However, the anticipated challenges such as culture shock, making new friends, new sports and foods, language barriers, the new education system among others made it seem impossible to actualize my "American dream" of one day becoming a student in one of the great American universities. I always hold on to the value of making the impossible possible, knowing very well that making a good choice is of equal importance since life is a function of choices. With that in mind, I started doing more research on colleges and universities in the United States of America, with a keen eye on what would perfectly fit my values and beliefs and not to deviate from my uniqueness.

I later found out about Historically Black Colleges and Universities (HBCUs) in the US. My dad attended a conference in Florida and later traveled to Baltimore, Maryland to visit friends who told him all about Morgan State University, a HBCU in Baltimore. When my dad returned to Kenya, he encouraged me to find out more about Morgan State University and to consider applying for a master's degree there. As curious as I have always been, I made an initiative to research more about the institution and the course that would fit my future goals and objectives. I applied and lucky enough I got admission to Morgan State University to seek a master's degree in international Studies.

At the time I didn't really appreciate the concept of HBCUs; my main motivation was simply to attend a college in the US, which now I had the chance to. It was only when I arrived on campus in Fall 2019 that I fully understood what HBCUs have to offer. I was taken aback by the racial demographics at Morgan State. From the classroom to my student accommodation, the African

American community was represented at every level. This was exciting to me because it meant I could immerse myself fully in college life without ever feeling like my skin color made me stand out. To me this was the honeymoon phase of culture shock because of the excitement with one of them being the fact that I saw more people with the same skin color I had, the unique food, efficient systems (from check ins, communications, deliveries among others). I was also impressed with how people respect time, their friendliness, and the unique American accent.

Throughout my stay in the US, I have undergone several cross-cultural exchanges that have to some extent influenced my beliefs hence changing my life trajectory. I observed that several students are confident when expressing themselves. Most of them even in my class would indicate their academic challenges without the fear of being judged. This has helped me to become more confident within the country particularly with regards to how I approach my studies and how I interact with my lecturers. I am now able to express myself confidently especially in my class up to the extent of getting the confidence to stand up for a student leadership position.

During the pandemic, when the world seemed to be at a standstill and most of our classes paused for a while, I decided to make effective use of my time through networking. I was able to reach out to notable figures in Kenya and the USA such as Dana Balter (former Democratic Party Nominee for New York's congressional district 24) who agreed to my request of being guests on my online youth empowerment platform. I initiated the Youth Empowerment Platform during the COVID pandemic in Fall 2020 where I invited dynamic leaders such as Dr. David Wachira, a World Bank Finance Specialist to speak to the Kenyan youth on various empowerment programs. These are ideas that were influenced by my exposure and connections that I made in the US. My immersion into American culture was realized through attending several events such as Thanksgiving where I learnt more about American culture. I remember I celebrated my first Thanksgiving in Syracuse, New York with my friend, Heather Waters, a Town Councilor in Manlius.

However, I struggled initially with having a different accent. I often had to back up my speech with gestures and signs to avoid misunderstanding. It also took me a while to understand that words may mean different things in the US compared to what I was used to in Kenya. I remember one day I ordered chips and a Coke in a restaurant because that was all I recognized on the menu – only to be presented with a bag of crisps. I had been expecting French fries because we call them chips in Kenya. That was a little bit embarrassing.

As time went on, I began to overcome some of these challenges. I attended a lot of campus activities with domestic students, which helped me acclimatize to the accent and culture. I also began working in the bookstore on campus, which enabled me to interact with lots of different people. I also got a graduate assistantship program where I mainly tutored students and worked in the languages department hence constantly enhancing my interactions. Outside university, I've traveled to many places in the US, such as New York, Ohio, and Illinois, which was another useful way to widen my exposure to American culture.

At the US Department of National Treasury with Senator Moses Kajwang of Kenya (left) and Deborah Crane (center), the Director for African Office, the US department of National Treasury

Once I had settled into university life, I ran for the position of international students' representative on the graduate student association and got elected. In this role I developed a scheme to help international students transition easily into a new culture by pairing them up with domestic students. I have found that Morgan State offers a lot of support for international students, particularly in terms of funding. For instance, I only had to pay tuition fees in full for the first semester and have received scholarships and graduate assistantships for the remaining semesters. After talking to other international students, this level of support seems quite common at HBCUs.

I also recently joined a project run by the deputy vice-president of international affairs to help drive international student recruitment in Kenya, which is a further example of Morgan's commitment to its international student community. Even though there were some slight challenges and culture shock in the beginning, the support available to help you settle in eases the change significantly.

On reflection, I know I made the right choice with Morgan State

University. I would encourage any prospective international student who dreams of studying in the US to apply to an HBCU. Based on my experience, culture shocks will always exist, and the best way of approaching them is through getting a mentor who will help in the process of culture immersion, networking, and making friends.

This article was first published in January 2022 by the Times Higher Education, a British magazine reporting specifically on news and issues related to higher education.

COLLINS OSWAGO (from Kenya) is a Graduate Student pursuing a Master's Degree in International Studies with a concentration in International Business and Development. Collins currently serves as the International Student's representative. His major research interest is in governance and development in Africa. Email: coosw1@morgan.edu

27

Becoming a Morganite

Abubakar S. Ringim, *Nigeria*

I still remember that day when my department head, Prof. Musa M. Dogara, made a phone call asking me if I still have interest in studying at Morgan State University. I said, "yes!" because I foresaw myself as a Morganite. For a long time, I found a truth in this statement: *The mind is everything. What you think, you become* – Buddha. As a nature enthusiast, I longed to visit the United States because of its vast wilderness areas. While learning has been a consistent journey in my life, it is sometimes challenging yet fascinating. This is especially true when the learning environment is entirely far away from where you live or know. The diverse cultures, norms and ethnicities in America particularly offer unique but fascinating experiences and challenges. However, my prior experience of venturing out into social and professional environments has encouraged me not to be wary of that.

I was full of excitement to start studying in America. Everything had been different in September 2020, when I officially started the PhD program in bioenvironmental science. The Coronavirus pandemic affected my immediate travel to the United States, though, because most activities had to succumb to global shut down. After a few weeks of online lectures from Nigeria, I become nervous trying to adjust and get used to the time differences (5 – 6 hours) and working styles. At the beginning of this exciting journey, I had to opt out for a course because the lecture time is 12 am - 3 am in Nigeria. Also, it was not easy to constantly keep track of homework and other deadlines on the new learning tool – Canvas. Sometimes I submitted an assignment at the last minute, or when the date completely passed, woe!

As the weeks pass, I become increasingly confident and more comfortable because the tutors were very friendly, patient, and compassionate. Dr. Jonathan Wilson was among the tutors who always keep the class fun and engaging. There were many instances where they extended the assignment deadlines, adjusted the lecture timetable, or shifted mid-term exams to accommodate everyone, especially international students like me. Interestingly, many of the tutors became mostly available to meet and discuss issues with students. And, since lectures are held online, they are recorded and uploaded online so that one can watch later time, or date. This was rather an unusual experience to see how enthusiastic and supportive the tutors were to see us through our academic goals. My cohort has also been very instrumental and supportive and before I knew it, we became one family. My friends from the United States in particular, Tameka Taylor, helped me become familiar with many norms of the foreign land.

Collectively, these experiences made me feel that I am part of a bigger, loving family of Morganites. What impressed me the most is whenever I mentioned that I am from Nigeria, many asked me wow, from Nigeria! Nigeria is reputed as the most populous black nation in the world and the giant of Africa. Like the United States, for instance, Nigeria is incredibly blessed with diverse culture and ethnicity, with some 300 ethnic groups. Eventually, this wonderful experience came to an end when I wrote my Fall 2020 examinations. Although the holiday was not long, the Spring semester 2021 comes with its lovely experience, too, because it is at this stage that the Program Coordinator Dr. Chunlei Fan advised us to look out for potential advisory members for the dissertation projects. By the end of the Spring semester, I had finished the exams – coursework with particularly good grades and formed a dissertation committee as well.

Presently, I am in the second year working on the dissertation titled Human Dimensions of Sika Deer Management. My advisory members, notably Dr. Scott Knoche and Kaitlynn Ritchie (pictured below) of the Patuxent Environmental and Aquatic Research Laboratory (PEARL) at MSU are incredibly supportive and provide guidance in this exciting project. Over the past six months of online meetings and discussions, we got Institutional Review Board approval to start data collection in November 2021.

My dissertation committee members. From left to right: Kaitlynn Ritchie, Dr. Scott Knoche (*Chair*), and me

On the 7th day of February 2022, this exciting journey began to take a new shape when at 9:25 am I departed for the United States from the Nmandi Azikiwe International Airport, Abuja. You know what? This was the first time I left Africa (I have been to about six countries in Africa, though), and as such, I am full of awe to have adventures. Over the course of this journey, we crossed the vast Sahara Desert – the largest desert in the world, mostly over much of Algeria, before crossing the Mediterranean Sea, and finally into Europe. The Mediterranean Sea separates Africa and Europe where we flew over the mountainous region in Andorra, as captured below.

Around 14:45 on the same day, we arrived at Heathrow International Airport, United Kingdom. Heathrow is an incredibly busy airport having many tunnels and traffic lights; no wonder it tops the list of the busiest airports in the world. Meanwhile, without wasting much time, after boarding two electric trains, I rushed for my boarding pass because my connecting flight to Washington D.C. was scheduled to depart at 16:30. From the United Kingdom to North America, we crossed the vast Atlantic Ocean for more than three hours traversing around Iceland and into Greenland – the largest island in the world. At 20:10, we landed at Dulles International Airport, wow! I think you can feel how I felt! I was overwhelmed, I arrived in the United States.

At arrival, Scott is waiting to pick me up to head for PEARL, which is located a two-hour drive from Washington. On our way to PEARL, out of generosity, we stopped by a small shopping store where Scott bought a burger and drink for me. Around 22:35 pm, we finally arrived at PEARL, after an 18-hour journey. PEARL is situated within Jefferson Patterson Park and Museum, along the Patuxent River in the Chesapeake Bay, St. Leonard. It is in this serene environment that I will stay conducting social science research, including work related to non-native species management for the next fifteen months or so.

In the United States, I much anticipated encountering cross-cultural experiences, especially related to food. The fact that I live remotely in the countryside, I knew it is not possible to get a food cuisine I am used to in Nigeria, even though there are a few places I heard in Baltimore serving Nigerian foods, but they are far from PEARL. Therefore, I prepared to become a cook, and this reminds me of those good days I spent in Tanzania during my master's program. Two days after arriving and trying to acclimate to the unique environment (as pictured below) Kaitlynn took me for shopping in Giant and Walmart that are like the Nigeria's Shoprite where I bought a lot of food, as if we are going to have a party at PEARL. I said to Kaitlynn, "I bought a lot of stuff that can last me for a couple of weeks, or months including bread, rice, macaroni, tomatoes, apples, onions, cowpea, grapes, sardines, corn flakes, oats, sugar, salt, garlic, garlic spice, turmeric, cinnamon, and others."

Amazingly, I could not get Maggi seasoning which is widely common and crucial in food preparation in Nigeria. In comparison to Nigeria, it is salt commonly used instead of Maggi seasoning in the United States. Kaitlynn informed me that I can order it from Amazon - wow something that is badly common even in corner shops in Nigeria. Unbelievably, I bought an adapter for $10 in Walmart (which just cost less than $2 in Nigeria) to enable me to charge my phones because we used plug types D and G in Nigeria, whereas A and B are obtainable in the United States.

On our way back Kaitlynn stopped by Chipotle where we bought a Burrito – a kind of food consisting of a flour tortilla wrapped into a sealed cylindrical shape around various ingredients including rice, beans, pepper, and other condiments. What a nice food experience! We also bought tortilla chips made with corn masa flour, like the common pringles I know except that it is not very salty.

The next cross-cultural experience I had was also on visiting Gateway restaurant with Scott and his wife Rebecca along with their children: Henna, Benjamin, and Leah. They invited me and my Nepalese friend Shivish for dinner. This countryside restaurant is popular for its local cuisine and sea foods. It was surprising to see that unlike in northern Nigeria where I came from, it is a norm for families to eat in public. Although I am not familiar with most food types on the menu, I ordered fried shrimp and coleslaw. Sea foods are exceedingly rare in northern Nigeria, and most people do not consume it due to ethical or cultural grounds, but I am used to sea foods because of my experiences in Tanzania. While having some fascinating conversion in Gateway, Rebecca narrated her wonderful cultural experiences during her two-year work in Senegal, West Africa in the late 2000s.

Another interesting experience is that unlike English speakers in Nigeria, people in the United States speak with different accents, and this made me remember the wacky phone call I had with the Social Security office the week I arrived where it took them 3 - 4 minutes to correctly get the spellings of my surname. I also realized that people here smile more frequently and are ever ready to wave or say "hello," "hi", "how are you" at the first meeting, irrespective of the individual's age or gender. It is amazing to see that most of the houses built in the US are made from wood, occasionally supported with red bricks but not concrete or blocks as in Nigeria. Unlike in Nigeria, particularly in the north, vultures are extremely rare, but seeing a lot of Turkey vultures soaring in the sky in the US proved to me that I truly live on the other side of the world. Vultures in Nigeria are killed for bushmeat and for use in traditional medicine, which is not the case in the United States highlighting different cultural values. I am optimistic that a lot of cross-cultural experiences and adventures would unfold often during my stay in the United States. Of particular interest, I would love to visit the first National Park in the world, the Yellowstone, Grand Canyon National Park, Nebraska wetland, Missouri Botanical Garden, and the Natural History Museum, as well as other captivating places.

To sum up, without a doubt, studying in the United States and especially at MSU has improved my skills and my perception about the other side of the world. Studying here in MSU has freedom and a sense of belonging and respect irrespective of one's religion, ethnicity, or culture. In general, being part of the Morgan family has further sharpened my understanding about the good student-teacher relationship. On a personal note, I enjoyed meeting and socializing with folks from diverse backgrounds. Scott Knoche and Kaitlynn Ritchie are generous, supportive, and they work to make me feel comfortable in the United States and I owe them a debt of gratitude. I am proud of my country for offering me the opportunity to study in the United States under the Tetfund-Morgan bilateral agreement. I am indebted to Prof. Hakeem I. Tijani. Until I graduate, my fingers are crossed to see what this land of opportunity has for me.

ABUBAKAR S. RINGIM is a graduate research assistant at PEARL. He holds a B.Sc. Zoology and M.Sc. Biodiversity Conservation from Bayero University Kano in Nigeria and University of Dar es Salaam Tanzania, respectively. Before coming to the United States, he was based at Federal University Dutse where he taught courses related to ecology and biodiversity conservation. He was also involved in national and regional conservation activities in, for example, the Nigerian Bird Atlas Project, and REDISSE Project, and he is a member of the Nigerian Coordination Group of Key Biodiversity Areas. He serves as Head of Biodiversity Conservation and Education Unit in the Centre for Arid Zone Ecologyn and he was one of the co-founders and Secretary Federal University Dutse Conservation Society (2018-date).

28

A New Culture: A New Style of Learning

Freda Alabi, *Nigeria*

Living and studying in America has been a completely transformative experience. To acculturate to a new environment is equivalent to embarking on a life-transforming journey that requires a lot of patience and discipline. The intellectual challenge of adjusting to both the cultural demands of life in America and a totally different style of teaching and learning in schools, foreign to what you are accustomed to, can be an overwhelming experience. I have had a transforming experience after arriving in the United States from Nigeria to pursue my graduate degree.

On arrival in the states, I had difficulty understanding the accent of people, and they had difficulty understanding my accent also. Not only did the accents make communication difficult, but the spelling of common words and the use of common words were a source of constant confusion. Since Nigeria was colonized by the British, I was used to the British way of spelling and pronunciation of words. For example, I used the British conventions for spelling words such as labour, honour, or colour. Often, my American professors would correct my spelling to the American versions of the words, i.e., labor, honor, and color. I had to remember to double-check my spelling before submitting my work. Also, I had to learn to switch from using words like "boot" of a car or torch to the American synonyms for those words, trunk and flashlight. I recall referring to the trunk of my car as "boot" in a conversation with a friend, and she had no idea what I was talking about.

Teaching and Learning in the United States

I also quickly realized how different the style of teaching and learning was here in the states compared to the lecture method that was widely used in our Nigerian schools. However, as a Nigerian, I have seen and had a fair share of new and frightening experiences that pushed me to remodel myself. As a child, I watched my mother build a teaching career and family, starting from an associate degree to a Ph.D. from one of Nigeria's foremost universities. My mother grew up in an era where educating a girl child was not popular. While her brothers went to colleges to study medicine, law, and engineering, she was given the basic high school education and thereafter married at 18. However, I watched my mother surpass the limitations placed on her by her culture to attain educational and professional heights beyond her more exposed siblings. She happens to be the only Ph.D. holder in our family.

My mother's achievements inspired me as a young woman and built a firm resolve in me to reach far and beyond my comfort zone. She inspired my initial decision to take up teaching in Nigeria for eight years, introducing me to this fascinating world of having the privilege of contributing to the development of young lives. After earning a bachelor's degree in chemistry, I realigned my interest in education to equip myself with the technical tools I needed to make significant contributions to the education sector. This focus fueled my ambition to pursue a master's degree in the United States, despite my anxiety about moving to the U.S.

The mental adjustment of switching cultures and starting life afresh in an unfamiliar place brought on a lot of uncertainty. Having lived all my life around family and a known culture, embarking on a journey so far away from home and in a culture completely different from mine added to my unease. I struggled with the anxiety of fitting in socially and academically. I felt unsure if my culture would be accepted and respected. These numerous concerns compounded my anxiety. Furthermore, part of my academic uneasiness was mainly about the style of learning, which was very different from what I was accustomed to.

The Nigerian education system used and continues to use a didactic approach to teaching–relying primarily on lecturing. Learning entails listening and answering questions when asked and memorization of lessons. Furthermore, professors are highly revered and unapproachable in most cases. This is unlike the United States, where I heard that the graduate programs often involve a great deal of reading and writing, and students are expected to engage in research and presentation of original ideas. Also, participation and discussions are highly encouraged. These were learning styles I had not explored in my years of learning.

After arriving in the U.S. and settling into classes, most of my fears and anxiety came alive. Half of the time, I was confused and behind in class work because I was yet to adjust to the new teaching style. My resolve to reach beyond my comfort zone gave me the resilience to push through the first semester of my master's program without quitting. During subsequent semesters, I got more comfortable and was able to make connections with other students. I joined study groups and took advantage of the resources available within the school. As I made connections and built relationships with the people around me,I gained friends who feel more like family to me. The people around me learned a lot about my culture and respected it, and I learned a lot about American culture. We realized how unique our different cultures were while also finding commonalities that strengthened our appreciation for one another and our cultures. After earning my master's degree, the passion for contributing to education by effecting positive changes in teaching and learning was part of what drove me to pursue a doctorate in science education.

From Behaviorist to Constructivist Theories of Learning

My perspective about learning and teaching has evolved through the course of my doctorate program at Morgan State University. I have had the opportunity to unlearn a lot to learn what the true definition of learning is. It has been a journey of re-invention of who I am, how I learn, and what my role is in impacting the Nigerian educational system. My learning experience growing up, which formed the background of my teaching experience is the behaviorist view of learning. This view of learning assumes that the student is essentially passive and responds to environmental stimuli and the behavior of a learner is shaped through positive and negative reinforcement (Schunk, 2020). For me, this is the only culture of education I knew. My learning was greatly influenced by cues and reinforcements. I never understood what it meant to make meaning of my learning experiences or to engage in metacognition.

In the course of this program, it began to be clear that knowledge is a function of how a person makes meaning from their experiences, and we cannot defend and apply learning until we have made sense of it. This resonates strongly with the constructivist view of learning. The purpose of learning in this model is for an individual to construct their own meaning, not to memorize what is handed down from their experiences with the given subject matter. Information can be received passively but understanding must come from making meaningful connections between prior knowledge, new knowledge, and the different learning processes (Liu et al., 2010). This paradigm of learning has enhanced my understanding of learning in various ways. It makes sense to me that learning should be fun, collaborative, occur in a real-world context, and must involve practice. As an educator, I tend to strongly resonate with the constructivist view of learning.

Though learning during my educational journey has been deeply rooted in behavioral learning theories, I have always advocated for a more student-centered approach to learning. The challenge has always been the gap between theory and practice for teachers like me who did not know how to use it effectively in the classroom. I am unlearning and re-learning how to better construct knowledge as a student, as well as understanding my role as a teacher to be that of a facilitator and co-partners with my students in their learning process. Thus, becoming a better version of a good educator in comparison to my background of learning.

Looking Back

America has become a home to me. I look back and am proud of this culture-shift journey I embarked on. I can affirm that the best decisions are moving to the U.S. and pursuing my doctorate at Morgan State University, a Historically Black University. I am now more confident and comfortable with the learning culture in the states and have made meaningful connections with my professors and classmates. With the support of my professors, friends, and classmates, my aspiration and passion for effecting positive changes the way our children are taught. This passion inspires me to constantly seek transformation through innovative approaches to teaching and learning.

References

Schunk, D. (2020). *Learning theories: An educational perspective* (8th ed.). Pearson.
Liu, C. C., & Chen, I. J. (2010). Evolution of constructivism. *Contemporary Issues in Education Research, 3*(4), 63. https://doi.org/10.19030/cier.v3i4.199

FREDA ALABI (originally from Nigeria) is a doctoral student in the Urban Educational Leadership Program in the School of Education and Urban Studies. Her major research interests lie in teaching and learning in science, instructional leadership, and educational policy. Email: froko2@morgan.edu

29

My Experience as an International Student in America

Otily Toutsop, *Cameroon*

I am originally from Cameroon and am currently a fourth-year doctorate student. I flowered the United States soil precisely in 2016. That date will be eternally engraved in my brain. I imagined myself as a part of the cosmos, or, to put it another way, as if I were living in a paradise on earth since I was so happy to have landed in Uncle Sam's nation, as most people call to the North American continent—not knowing what to look forward to in terms of the reality of the field at this point. My time with my family had been quite pleasant, but the real tragedy began when it became absolutely required to attend school. Here I am, rushing to the bus station to catch the first bus of the day. I had to manage with coins because I didn't yet have a valid bus ticket for the entire month. A situation that was still manageable given the circumstances.

My primary source of frustration was not memorizing the bus stop locations and how to transfer to the second bus to get to school. It took me approximatively three hours to get to school on a journey that regularly takes forty-five minutes. On the bus, most of the passengers were staring at me, and I found myself becoming agitated by the looks of other passengers. I was frequently irritated with myself for not knowing where I was going. For example, once, on my way back to school, I was halted by a lot of snow, and I found myself crying and trying to figure out how to catch the next bus. Honestly, it was the most terrible day of my life since I ended up with frozen hands that were nearly motionless due to the experience. I sobbed all evening and berated myself for traveling to America.

The first institution I attended was predominantly white, with fewer than one percent of Black students. Coming from a nation where socialism and charity were instilled in me as a child, I was taken aback by realizing that I had landed in a universe of individuality. It was a challenging world for me to confront and adjust to. The educational system in my nation encourages students to work together and exchange ideas to better grasp the teachings taught by their professors.

However, earning a scholarship of up to $80,000 to continue studying at that time at a predominantly white institution changed my vision. Psychologically, I wanted to attend a Black institution right away to meet my people. Fortunately for me, I was accepted into the engineering program at Morgan University, where I continued my master's degree program with a scholarship that I received almost immediately.

During my first week back at Morgan, I was impressed by the overwhelming presence of Black students on the university campus. The university's president and most administrative personnel were of African descent. My best moment at Morgan was when I joined the Center for Reverse Engineering Assurance Microelectronics Center (CREAM) to pursue my thesis. I would also like to recognize that my advisor did an excellent job supporting my research.

My second most significant difficulty was adjusting to American society, particularly the cuisine. Every neighborhood in the city has several food restaurants that specialize in well-known fast meals such as pizza, for the most part. For example, when I had pizza for the first time in 2017, my tongue rejected it since it was unfamiliar. So far, my eating habits have not drastically changed, and I continue to discover new dishes every day as I travel to other places.

Moreover, I was also upset by the change in temperature, which was unfamiliar to me and made it particularly difficult to live in. Where I originate from, there are only two primary seasons: the dry and the wet. I had never seen snow before arriving in America, and the first snowfall forced me to stay at home for over a week without stepping outside.

When summer arrived, I was relieved that everything would improve and be able to return to the climate that I was familiar with. Unfortunately for me, the rapid rise in warmth had almost caused my delicate black skin to break. Particularly when it became essential for me to stand at bus stops to sit down and wait for the bus to pass. I also realized very soon that I needed to improve my ability to endure since I had no option.

My most excellent source of inspiration at the time was the desire to constantly put up my best effort to attain my goals. I always told myself that I wanted to be the one that encourages the next generation to strive for more extraordinary things. No matter how difficult life gets, my excitement is that my tale will be used to help someone else one day. I've always had the goal of turning my mistakes into opportunities for growth.

I ultimately realized that the only way to better understand this new existence was to experience numerous failures.

I want younger generations to learn about the importance of endurance through my story. Some challenges prepare us for a better future that we cannot see right now. As a teenager, I realized early on that life is about tenacity, no matter where we live. Success can only be achieved through hard work. My grandma always says, "persuade yourself that the future is full of surprises no matter the difficulties." To everybody who reads my tale, I encourage you to always do your best, no matter how challenging life becomes. The road ahead will be complex, but only perseverance will get us through to victory. Conviction and ongoing drive will enable us to cope better with the uncertain nature of the future. Using successful people as role models can give us the confidence to achieve our goals no matter what obstacles we face.

--

OTILY TOUTSOP, originally from Cameroon, is a doctoral student in the Department of Electrical and Computer Engineering at Morgan State University, Maryland. E-mail: ottou1@morgan.edu

30

Amelican Palava: Words, World, or Wonder

Jennifer Umezinwa, *Nigeria*

The ravaging thoughts in my mind at that point kept wandering from the reason for my throbbing headache to the possibility of hearing a loud, *"yo black girl, go back to Africa!"* from a racially intolerant pedestrian on the streets of Baltimore. Nonetheless, I stood up from the seat at the rest area where I had been sitting and thinking for the past three hours. I eventually summoned the courage to let my host know I had arrived at Baltimore-Washington International Airport. I heard two shrieked voices in the background. *Yayy, Jenny is here!* As soon as I heard the little voices in the background from the other end of the call, I gained a little motivation and smiled. I thought to myself, maybe I had eventually found another place that I could call home. The best voice in my head kept telling me this trip was a good decision. Another tinkling noise yelled back at the still voice, girl! You are in for a ride. Well, I guess they were both right.

****

I remember checking my emails on my white reading table in my white-painted house before sleeping on my new pink Mickey Mouse bedspread. *Colored.* I had shopped for a new bedspread like I do every three months. The idea of sleeping in something new gave me the hope of dreaming one more time about the future I had imagined for myself. Not that the new sheet would take me to the dream world where I live the life I envision, but you know, just that girlish fantasy… maybe clairvoyance. Waking up for me is quite different from getting up from my bed. I was eyes wide awake, but I knew my legs could not get any further from their curled position in the middle of my bed. What sprang me up was the 12th of the frequent notifications that had been beeping. They kept coming in, at least every three seconds in the next two minutes. What could these notifications be about? Your guess is as good as mine. By the time I returned to my little home office, the white reading table set, there were eight emails from one sender. I remember the sender's name from when I turned in my application to study for a Ph.D. degree in English at Morgan State University, Maryland, U.S.A. What information necessitated eight emails at once! The first one read, "Congratulations, you have just been offered admission into …." Then… I had a bird eye view of what was contained in the rest of the seven emails. For another 15 seconds, my world stopped. I could not react, think, or move. Could it be a premonition of an apocalypse or my dreams coming true? I summoned the courage to open the second email, and the third… and the eight, all emails concerning my studentship. Then I smiled…then I laughed, and laughed, and screamed, and jumped, and kept jumping. Then I started dancing and singing and thanking God. But I pinched myself, knocked on wood to be sure I was awake, then I went back to the email to read again. This time, I sat on my white chair with my legs crossed. My efforts and aspirations flashed before my eyes. My eyes, for some reason, had begun to produce a generous amount of salty H20. I was happy and at the same time, confused. Confused, I was about who to contact first, the email sender or my family. Fast forward to my visa interview amidst COVID.

****

Time, like people, was scarce. Time raced fast, just like people moved swiftly and far while observing social distance. I wish I could buy some company or time as I sat across from the booth facing my interviewer, a white, tall, lanky American. Of all the questions he asked, the one that struck me the most was why I chose Morgan State University. While I considered my response, I analyzed the purpose for the question. I gave him three reasons, and he told me that what stood out for him was my consideration of an academic community where I can identify with people with whom I share real-world cultural experiences. I got the visa to travel immediately. I fled from the embassy, seeing that I had crunch time to plan my trip.

****

As soon as my ride pulled up, my tensed nerve began to cool off just a little bit. I was still anxious about a world away from family, friends, job, and the white home space I unwillingly left behind. My ride from Washington DC to Baltimore was cold and quiet. I was fascinated by the tall trees with no leaves. I compared the trees here with those juicy trees that grow different fruits back home and how my siblings and I used to eat off those mango, orange, coconut, and pawpaw trees in my parent's orchard behind our house. My dad plucked from the banana and plantain trees. He never agreed with the idea of females getting close to those two trees so that we do not alter their cycle of growth. For us, that mystery is understood only by him. My love for fresh foods started getting in the way of my already calm nerves. I knew I was acting up in arms. I looked at my hands and legs, and they were moving to the same rhythm of my heartbeat, music that sounded like fear and uncertainty.

****

Three days later, I had recovered from the jetlag. I also recovered from the sessions of blank-mindedness and summoned the courage to pray again. After my long chat with Kaka about my experiences so far, I heard *Kaka* (grandma) say *I am so happy to hear your voice but, eishhhh... Amelican Palava!* Kaka still tells me to try to speak my native language often in order not to contribute to language loss of my dialect. Half the time I spent sitting on my new black reading set, I would reflect on how God created different people with thick or light hair, rhotic or dense accents, and many such unique identities. I felt like a drop in a mighty ocean. You know... there was another unsettling thought in my head. Did I deserve this level of success, or did I get here by the skin of my teeth? More rewarding, as I sat still, I grew determined to hit the books and be sure to prove myself. My mind got free and clear as the months went by. I still reminisce on how God has been there for me. I have new friends, family, culture, a new ash-colored space that did not seem different from what I left behind. Though I still wish I could travel with the room space that I owned back home if wishes were horses, or my pink bedspread, the little things that girls want. And because I never forget where I came from as I continue to picture where I am going...

JENNIFER ANULIKA UMEZINWA (Originally from Nigeria) is a doctoral student in the Department of English, School of Liberal Arts. Her major interests lie in Linguistics, American Diasporic Literary Criticism, and English Composition. Email: jeume1@morgan.edu

31

Resilience! My Watchword in My New Home

Bukola Daramola, *Nigeria*

My determination to study in America is one that kept me and everyone around me wondering how and where I got the strength to accomplish it: being a mother of three children, married, with a career as a registered nurse and a public health expert working and living in Nigeria which is my place of birth. I had a master's in health and safety education from the prestigious University of Ibadan, Nigeria and had done my induction to commence a PhD program, yet I left all in quest for knowledge that I believed is holistic and more than what I could acquire in my country.

I came to the US for the Fall 2019 semester to study family and consumer science (human sciences) at a graduate level from Prairie View A&M University, Texas. On arrival at the airport, I was conveyed into the school campus by the president of the Nigeria Student Association of that institution, a union I later became its secretary. Prior to coming, I had made friends with two female students from my country studying in the same institution, who had gone out of their way to make accommodation arrangements and lots more for me. They became my sisters and guardian as I journeyed in my new home. The first shock I had was seeing the landlord put a lock on my door a month after I came because I couldn't pay my rent when due. I had exhausted all the dollars I came with immediately to settle my tuition, rent, and groceries. I needed to exchange naira (Nigeria currency) to dollars to pay rent which was delaying, then I was told that delaying bill payment in America is a thing I must plan to face the aftermath. Thank God my room was unlocked after I successfully made the payment.

Registration hustle was not too challenging, discussing and listening to my classmates was the greatest challenge I encountered academically. The faculties were patient enough to ask me to repeat myself, but my collogues were not and seriously, I was not hearing them either. After a while I developed a defense mechanism by telling them to always repeat what they said, and they later learnt from me that I was having the same difficulty hearing their spoken English the same way they have difficulty hearing me. I had no choice I kept discussing in class against all odds to maintain a good grade of A which I did in my courses.

After staying for two months in the school, income from home could no longer support me. I had to look for a job. I applied for several jobs posted on the school website, and I attended several interviews with no job secured, I had to seek to work in the school cafeteria (SODEXO), what humbled me most was the nagging attitudes of some of the supervisors who didn't want to understand the differences in my cultural background. I could remember crying when going home from work and asking myself if the price I'm paying is worth it. One of the faculties that saw my resume while applying for job asked why I was doing a second master instead of the PhD. This along with my resilient nature made me to apply for doctoral study in public health. I was admitted and commenced the program in fall 2020. I later secured a graduate assistant job before the end of the Fall 2019 semester. This was a huge milestone in my settling in my new home, far away from home.

My relocating to Maryland from Texas can only be explained by my resilient nature-- it was like when I first came to the America. I knew no one in my new school Morgan State University, I had no job, and no funds were forth coming from home because of the effect of the pandemic. I rented a room and packed in to face the academic year ahead. Then came the issue of finances and bill payment. I was almost dropped from school due to inability to pay my tuition, but God was gracious to me. I got a research assistant job before the school dropped date. Doing my desired course, doctoral public health and my new job made encouraged me to be the best I could ever be. My GPA in Fall 2020 semester as a doctoral student was 4.00, with all As in my four courses. I was awarded a Featherstone HBCU scholarship in April 2021 which was applied for my tuition in 2021 and 2022. At this point, things were getting better for me in my new home. I have made friends and my church members Mercy Court RCCG have become a great community around me. My team at work in the Office of Academic Affairs has been super supportive. But all this gave me joy that lasts only when am around them. After I go back to my lonely and quiet room, I long to see my children and family. I travelled back to Nigeria in June 2021 on visitation for a month. My interaction with family, friends, and collogues demonstrated how fast my new home changed my reasoning, the way I relate with and appreciate people. My children and husband joined me in my new home in September 2021. Life has never remained the same. Indeed, resilience is key in my new home.

I composed this poem for my class group as our presentation in one of my courses: all four group members are Africa Immigrants.

African Immigrant Student

Like the rising of the sun, Strong as the move of a wave
Departing from everything that means so much to me,
To a world so desired but vague, Home far away from home,
To fulfill a desire that is burning in my heart, a quest for knowledge that cannot be hidden.

It was an indescribable excitement, with a bright and rejoicing soul.
Full of strength and occupied with the sweet memory of my childhood,
Where I hear the birds sing and the wave of the ocean tides,
With the sun shining bright on my skin to make it healthy and black,
And my companions looking out for me to do the usual that gladden the heart.

Then my dream comes true, my quest to acquire knowledge overpowers me,
I crossed to my new home far away from home,
Wow, what an enigmatic glamour, with giant buildings that kept me wondering if it was built by the gods,
My new home is adorable, with everything done at the speed of light.
my new world so desired but lonely,
Where I no longer hear the bird sing and see the wave of the ocean tides

Overwhelmed with the burden of making ends meet,
Faced with the financial onus that looks endless, yet no help rolling.
Making payment for daily necessity, with unending bills,
and no hope of where to make a living.
Being faced everyday with the fear of how to make my dream come true.

My desire for knowledge has become a burden,
 laden with unending communication from differs sources,
Lost in the center of my dream, captured in my new home far away from home,
Where do I go for help, who do I talk with to share my thought?
Who cares about what is happening in my mind and head?

My mind begins to long and desire for my home far away
Loneliness is now my companion and lack is my daily rhyme
My soul no longer rejoices, yet my cry for help cannot be heard,
Oh, what a time and season, where the healthy and strong are dropping,
 like a log of wood in the ocean.
likewise, the weak and fable are sleeping, never to wake up no more,

I look out for someone to share my burden,
Everyone is lock down and isolated in their homes,

I speak with voices and faces that I cannot touch, my breath is shortening due to constant covering of my nose without an end,
Everyone keeps a distance when talking to me,
Oh, what a season a time, so deadly and unending.

My dream though bright, my heart can no more bear,
My feet are heavy for lack of where to go,
My joy is mixed, seeing my quest for knowledge been achieved but my mind is solitary searching for the deep happiness in my new home
Oh, behold my tale, my pain and dilemma.

Then comes the cheerful news, the jingle of hope for my mind,
The excitement of a place where I can be heard and talk to, and a center that gather people of like passion as me,
I need to let someone knows, the benefit of sharing what is happening in their thought, mind, and head.
Come and be part of this, my friends from my new home so far away from home.

BUKOLA OMOTAYO DARAMOLA, is a foreign trained licensed Registered Nurse and Midwife, well-articulated and compassionate Public Health Professional, and a knowledgeable health educator with a strong work history in Maternal and Child Health among the disparity population. She obtained her Bachelors' and master's degrees in Health Education from Nigeria. She is currently a doctoral student in public health at Morgan State University, Baltimore. E-mail: budar2@morgan.edu

PART III
Cross Cultural Experiences of Faculty and Staff

32

Fulbright Narrative: The South African Experience

Adele S. Newson-Horst
Department of English & Language Arts

When I was an associate professor at Florida International University, I applied to the Fulbright Study/Research Program and was awarded a Fulbright Professorship in South Africa. I was assigned to teach at Potchefstroom University for Christian Higher Education (later renamed North-West University) from January through August 1993. It is one of five Afrikaans universities in the Republic of South Africa; it also has the distinction of being F.W. de Klerk's alma mater. My decision inspired a great deal of anxiety in my family, friends, and colleagues. Yet, at no time did I feel anxious over my decision. And perhaps it was because of this back of anxiety that my sojourn in South Africa proved to be the enriching experience that it was. I use the word "enriching" because even now, I cannot provide a definitive, qualitative statement on the experience.

The Social Experience
The University is situated in Potchefstroom, a small, conservative town in the Western Transvaal, some 118 kilometers southwest of Johannesburg. The town boasts the existence of the longest oak-lined lane in the Southern Hemisphere. The dominant vegetation is the thorn bush/tree. The architecture is a mix of Dutch cape buildings and what, for lack of a better word, I call nouveau African buildings—stucco constructions with high ceilings. The town is nestled between koppies (small hills) that dot the landscape. The landscape is dry---the community has experienced a seven-year drought which left the Mooi River that runs through town nearly dry. Yet, the effect is one of stark beauty and calm.

It was weeks before I discovered one of its many features that engaged my unconscious mind and linger yet today: "Uniformity." The town has the "sameness" flavor reminiscent of the midwestern United States of the 1950s. People are marked by uniforms. School children wear uniforms. The Afrikaner school girls parade about in a variety of pastels and the African school girls wear the requisite black jumpers with white blouses. The workers wear uniforms. Domestic workers are identifiable by jumpers of blue or pink stripes intermixed with white; they don these over their street clothes. On their heads, they are fond of wearing tams and scarves. Black laborers wear blue overalls, and their white bosses wear a khaki-colored or beige outfit of shorts and long socks. One never has to wonder about a person in passing him/her on the streets.

It was not long before all segments of Potchefstroom knew who I was and what I was doing there. They were, in the main, friendly and curious people, if not a bit status conscious. Whenever the town's people encountered me on the streets, they would invariably ask me about my church. Salvation is very much on their minds. First, they questioned which church I attended. After my religious affiliation had been firmly established, they invariably asked if I had gone to church on Sunday and whether I enjoyed the service. I encountered the question so frequently that I began to imagine that it was the Afrikaaner counterpart to the phrase, "Have a good day."

I believe that I was the only Black person living in town. Someone told me that a "coloured" school teacher was in the process of buying a house in town, but I never met him or her. While apartheid had been legally repealed some three years before my arrival, it remained intact socially and economically. So to get the full picture of the town and its people, I alternated between attending mass at the Catholic churches in Ikegeng (the African township), Promosa (the coloured township), on remote farms in open-air services, and Potchefstroom (the white town).

In the African township, mass is said in Tswana. The Africans living in the area are predominantly Tswana people, although they speak any number of other African languages, including Zulu and Khosla. The service in the African township is by far the most exciting although it may last the better part of the morning and often well into the afternoon. In the coloured township, mass is said in Afrikaans. On the outskirts of town, there are large farms, owned by whites, where African families live (in mud huts) and work the farms of their bosses, much like the old plantation system of the South. On the farms, the mass is a mix of Southern African languages, depending on who is present, and masses are usually followed by a dining feast. In town, mass is said in English. But by no means is Potchefstroom a Catholic community. The University and the town have strong ties with the Gereformeerde Kerk and the Nederlandse Gereformeerde (the Calvinist churches to which the majority of Afrikaans speaking South Africans belong). The whites who attend Catholic Church in town are mostly Portuguese shop owners and their families.

There was a novel quality to the things that I did in Potchefstroom. But it's more than that. In the air, there was a kind of anticipation of something happening soon. While I was there many things happened, including the assassination of Chris Hani (general secretary of the South African Communist Party) and the death (from natural causes) of ANC leader Oliver Reginald

Tambo. Also while I was in Potchefstroom, the right-wing front (the folks front) marched down the town's main street to show their solidarity and to mobilize right-wing resistance to change. In addition to the everyday violence—social, economic, and political in nature--the AWB (Afrikaner Weerstandsbeweging, a right-wing para-military Afrikaner organization whose members often appear in uniforms with a swastika-like emblem) tested the limits of the law by disrupting a meeting at the World Trade Center. In the towns, on the farms, in the cities— people went about their business with the discomfort/excitement (depending on to whom I spoke) of the anticipation of something happening.

I, in turn, was regarded by all as a novelty. The Africans regarded me as colored and often asked where in Promosa did I reside. The coloureds regarded me as "foreign"—my positions on solidarity puzzled them. Didn't I understand that culturally and linguistically there is great distance between the Black Africans and the coloureds, perhaps a distance that may never be bridged. The whites regarded me as an anomaly, I'm sure. In the town, after learning that I was from Miami, one shopkeeper took to calling me "the Miami Vice Girl" and the name held.

The University Experience
During my Fulbright experience, Potchefstroom University for Christian Higher Education had an enrollment of some 9,000 students—5% African, coloured, Indian and Korean; 15% English heritage, and 80% Afrikaaner heritage. The university employed no Black professors. Officially, to teach at the university one has to be a Christian, and it also helped if one was male and of Afrikaaner heritage. And although the language of instruction for every unit on campus (except the English Department) was Afrikaans, everyone sspoke some English.

The day after I arrived in Potchefstroom, my department chair, Annette, came over with one of her daughters who would baby-sit while we ran errands. She opened my garage door where a university car was awaiting me. After my arrival the previous day, I made a point of avoiding that car because the steering wheel was affixed to the right side of the dashboard. I wondered if it would be possible to walk the duration of my stay in Potchefstroom. Annette insisted that I drive.

She was something of a celebrity in town. Well known and formidable, she had some very definite notions about progress and reform in education. She directed me to the local chemist, doctor's office, grocery store, and liquor store, among other places, and made introductions. Next, she directed me to the home of a woman who trains African women to be maids. This is where I first met Maria (my children called her by her African name "Mamokhuku"). Maria was close to middle age and spoke English very well. The going rate for live-in maids was something like Rand 250 a month (less than a hundred dollars). We settled on a monthly rate of R 550 plus room and board. Later, one of my neighbors chided me for the "exorbitant" pay. Didn't I know how much these people talk

107

and what did I think would happen when she (meaning Maria) told the other girls (meaning the town's domestic workers) about her salary? "No, Adele, you mustn't spoil them. They will only take advantage." At this point, I knew I was perceived to be innocuous. Who in the world would tell another Black woman something like this?

After taking Maria to my home, Annette and I proceeded to the University where the work began and did not end until of my departure. A prominent reason for the ease in adjustment at the University had to do with the immense duties assigned to me from day one. Ours was a small department (some 9 faculty members) with a large population of students. In the first year class alone, the student-lecturer ratio was 122:1. In addition to teaching, the faculty was expected to produce translations of reports for other campus units. Woefully overworked, my colleagues were happy to share the responsibilities.

I believe that we got on as well as we did because of the inordinate amount of work. And too, the tearoom phenomenon aided the process. Each day at 10:00 a.m., if not teaching, one was expected to show up for tea with the faculty from the Humanities and Modern Foreign Languages. At teatime, we would sit around a large room with tables in the middle discussing and sharing any number of ideas. Also, we celebrated birthdays and varied faculty successes at the end of each month by sharing in the consumption of homemade foods. Speechmaking was very much a part of these celebrations.

I taught a number of groups and courses, including a third-year research group, an honors course in American Poetry, an African American Literature course, and any number of lower-division seminars. The students were respectful and interested, although they were not inclined to contribute much to class discussions. This was particularly true of the first-year student who typically came from a family where Afrikaans is the language of the home and anything English is often viewed as suspect. One of my colleagues assured me that the Boer-English War is still raging.

I decided that education must be a chief value in the homes of these Afrikaaner students. I further decided that Annette had probably instilled the fear of God into these students. Additionally, my colleagues pointed out that the courses I taught were novelties. American literature was in some ways marginalized in South African universities. In fact, I was the first Fulbrighter in the discipline of English ever to teach at a South African university. In spite of their protests to the contrary, in some ways, the Boers were much colonized by the English. This is especially true in the Departments of English across the country where the canon and syllabus designs were almost entirely British in content.

Annette was instrumental in the recent change of name from the Department of English to the Department of English Language and

Literature. The name change suggested the range of activities in which the department engaged. Additionally, Annette was single-handedly responsible for the presence of the Black South African M.A. students in the department. While the undergraduate population of Africans was considerably low, the English Department had managed to attract Africans from across the country to engage in M.A. work in preparation for New South Africa. Moreover, because of the unrest on many of the Black University campuses, the more serious African students opted to matriculate at traditionally white institutions to achieve their ends. Over 50% of M.A. students in the English Language and Literature Department at Potchefstroom were African. I don't want to give the impression that this activity was the norm at the University, rather far from it. I saw little effort at recruitment in other departments.

I suppose that I was something of an oddity to most, which had the effect of making me well known on campus. In addition to invitations to tea from other departments, I frequently offered lectures to classes in psychology, philosophy, art history, etc. After work, the English Department faculty did a lot of socializing. Birthdays were very big events for the Afrikaaner, and the Sunday afternoon braai (bar-be-que) is something of a Boer institution. Additionally, I belonged to the Mooirivier Wynglide, a local wine guild, and I believe I was the first person of color to join the local fitness gym.

Other Experiences

The University provided me with a very spacious house on campus, rent, and maintenance free. The afternoon of the first full day of residence I was greeted by a neighbor who had baked some muffins for me and later received a visit from an elderly couple who lived on the block. I walked to campus after returning from my trek to the English Nursery each morning where I would leave my two children. My children became celebrities at the English-speaking nursery—the only one in town with a mixed-race clientele. Apparently, my son frequently employed the ruse of telling the other children that he would take them to America if they would give him the sweets in their lunches. My little girl was nicknamed "Miss America" because of her much remarked upon vanity and "elegant" social ways.

At any rate, the owner of the English Nursery was instrumental in enabling me to travel the country as much as I did. Usually, my children would stay with her and her family while I lectured at other institutions, including the Black Colleges (Fort Hare, University of the North, University of Venda, to name a few). On the occasion of Chris Hani's assassination, I happened to be in Windhoeck, Namibia, delivering lectures and opening an art exhibition. The news reports of the violence in response to the assassination was enough to convince me that the Republic of South Africa had been hurled into a full-scale civil war. Upon my return to South Africa, I sped from Jan Smuts Airport through Mid-Rand and Johannesburg, past SOWETO and to Potchefstroom in record time. I was met with roadblocks as I approached Potchefstroom but was not detained. I believe that the University car that I was driving (with emblem visible) was responsible for the ease with which I passed the roadblocks.

When I reached the English Nursery and my kids, it was as if nothing was happening. True the town was quiet—no commerce—and there was a notable lack of African presence, but there was no violence. My children's teacher explained to me that President De Klerk had deployed the military to surround and protect towns (read as white towns) upon the first signs of trouble. She further informed me that the Africans had called for a work stoppage, hence the lack of commerce and activity in the town. The activity in the townships, however, did not mirror the activity in town in any way. After retrieving my children, I went to Ikegeng for Maria. Maria told me that in the township schools were burning as well as automobiles; people were "toi-toing," and there was a sense of general chaos.

Apart from the people whom I befriended at the University and my children's teacher, I formed a friendship with a colored couple who also happened to have children the same ages as my own. Through them, I tried to understand the sentiment of separation from the Africans still espoused by many coloureds. Some coloureds were even arguing for their own homeland. I now believe that the phenomenon would take years of study to fully understand. But in addition to antagonism with Africans (the coloureds call the Africans "Kaffirs" while the Africans call the coloureds "Bushmen"), many coloureds are antagonistic toward Indians, for a number of reasons.

I recall telling the coloured couple about a conversation I had recently had with an Indian shopkeeper in town. According to the shopkeeper, we are all brothers and sisters, and Black pride was the only way to see us through the present crisis. The couple responded by asserting that the Indians in South Africa are opportunists with no real commitment to anything but amassing money and that now that change is in the air, they have formed alliances with the Africans. Furthermore, they pointed to the Indian leader of the Labour Union as an example, explaining that the vast majority of labourers in the country are African, and that the interest of the African labourer do not coincide with the interests of the Indian labourer.

The African students frequently visited me at my home at odd hours for tea and discussion. I never tired of hearing of their experiences. On one occasion, a student wanted desperately for me to understand how the African is viewed by the Boer, so he told me a story:

A Boer professor went to a bush school (African university) to teach geography. On the first day, one of the students in class raised his hand and asked, "Are you prejudiced, boss?" To which the professor replied that he was not. Another asked, "Well, would you permit me to marry your daughter?" The professor pondered on this a while and answered, "Why yes, I would." The same student then added, "And if we have children, would you welcome the children?" After more contemplation the professor responded, "The light ones I would welcome, the darker ones may work on my farm."

South Africa is a very complicated country with extremely complicated peoples. Contrary to what the media would have us believe, South African whites do not hold a monopoly on evil. Some, it seems to me are criminally ignorant about the effects of and the conditions inspired by apartheid. And many of the more educated Afrikaaners, it seems to me, are experiencing what James Baldwin called "subterranean Anglo-Saxon guilt" in relation to the Africans. Presently the country is faced with economic problems, political problems, and social problems that threaten to hurl it into a full-scale civil war. In addition to ethnic conflicts, indiscriminate violence is very much a reality in the township and larger cities. Attacks of an astoundingly vicious nature are reported regularly.

In the final report submitted to the Council for the International Exchange of Scholars, evaluating my professional and personal experience I wrote:

At this point, I am unable to evaluate or make meaning out of the dynamics of the interactions I had with the various people of South Africa. My interactions were intense and complicated, not unlike the country itself. If I thought that I understood this country before departing North America, my experiences suggest that I was mistaken. After eight months during which I bonded through working and socializing with the most unlikely people, a definitive statement of the experiences eludes me. About my experiences, I remain ambivalent.

Novelist Trey Ellis coined the phrase "cultural mulatto" to refer to African Americans who are able to navigate with ease through the worlds of Black and white expectations. Certainly African-American academics teaching at predominately white institutions of higher learning have had to become "cultural mulattos" out of necessity. The mechanism that enables the "cultural switching" also renders the individual to some degree innocuous—that mechanism, it seems to me, inspires ambivalence.

Postscript
Since my departure, the nation held its first full-participant, democratic, general election in 340 years. The African National Congress won the election with some 62.6% of the total votes, carrying seven of South Africa's nine new provinces. Nelson Rolihlahla Mandela now heads the first post-apartheid government, and outgoing President R. W. de Klerk serves as second deputy president.

Recently, I entertained an administrator from Potchefstroom (on a tour sponsored by the USIA) in my home. He reports that change is very much a fact of life in South Africa. In Potchefstroom alone, the schools in town are now multiracial, all of them. The town itself has seen the arrival of many African families. In nine months' time, Potchefstroom University for Christian Higher Education has moved from 5% enrollment of students of colour to a 10% enrollment, and the English Department alone has hired at least two persons of color as lecturers.

Violence remains very much a part of life in South Africa—deep seated racial and ethnic conflicts die hard. But, as my visitor told me, for those who remained, hope and optimism abound. And why not? According to columnist Raymond Louw,

> *It could be the last miracle of the 20ᵗʰ Century: an oppressed majority gaining it rightful place in the sun, not by enduring the horrors and chaos of bloody civil war—though the death toll in internecine fighting in the last 10 years has been an appalling 20,000— but by an almost unique process that can be described as "negotiated revolution." (Miami Herald, 24 April 1994, 1-C)*

President Mandela, himself, has proved to be something of a cultural mulatto.

Postscript 2022

Unbelievably, it has been almost two decades since my South African Fulbright experience. Yet it remains very vivid in my mind, the people, the sights, the smells, the sounds, and the amazing landscape that is the Republic of South Africa. Even today, based on speech, I can detect people (white and Black) from South Africa.

Nelson Mandela was released and became president from 1994 until 1999. He died on December 5, 2013. Bishop Desmond Tutu the anti-apartheid and human rights activist died on December 26, 2021. Both leaders had a hand in the Truth and Reconciliation Commission—the restorative justice body— assembled after the end of apartheid. Many view it as something of a failure because the members were not empowered to implement reparations.

Sometime later, I was able to see the parallels between apartheid and segregation in the US in a way I had never been able to do before. Activists contend that in America reparations and not reconciliation is needed.

Today, South Africa is as plagued by the Coronavirus as other countries throughout the world. Even before the advent of COVID, the country witnessed high rates of poverty, social inequality, unemployment, and public service access disparities that disproportionately affect black South Africans. Also, the deepening divisions and factionalism of the ANC is viewed as a threat to democracy. Its plight today is similar to that of the United States with deep divisions that threaten its security.

Note. This article was first published in *Sage*, Vol 9, No. 2 (Summer 1995), 63-66.

ADELE NEWSON-HORST is a Professor of English and coordinator of the Women, Gender, and Sexuality Studies Program at Morgan State University. Her research interests include African, Middle Eastern, African American, and Caribbean women writers. She earned the B.A. from Spelman College, the M.A. from Eastern Michigan University, and the Ph.D. from Michigan State University. Her books and articles focus on the literature of African, African American, and Caribbean women writers. She regularly reviews books for *World Literature Today* and *Academic Choice*. Among other publications, she has published two edited volumes on Egyptian novelist and physician Nawal El Saadawi: *The Essential Nawal El Saadawi: A Reader*, London, Zed Publishers, 2010 and The Dramatic Literature of Nawal El Saadawi, London: Saqi, 2009.

33

The Organizational Ombudsman and the Cross-Cultural Experience

Wilbur Hicks
Community College Leadership Program

It was my good fortune to work as an organizational ombudsman for three prominent organizations — Princeton University, the Shell Oil Company, and the International Monetary Fund. An organizational ombudsman is a confidential, neutral, independent, and informal resource that performs a number of roles in an organization. One of its primary roles is to assist the organization in responding to conflict. Each of these organizations wanted to confront the challenges involved in creating productive enterprises with diverse populations within their institutions. From my experiences in each of these organizations, I learned a great deal about racial, cultural, and religious differences and how they have the potential to both enhance and debilitate an organization.

My work as an organizational ombudsman began at Princeton University in New Jersey. After the O.J. Simpson trial, many U.S. colleges and universities exploded with protests about the climate, primarily racial, on their campuses. Many approaches were taken to respond to the student and faculty protests. Black Studies programs were introduced. The recruitment of faculty and staff of color was intensified. And the organizational ombudsman was introduced on many of these campuses. The idea of the ombudsman was to have a neutral, confidential, informal, and independent resource for members of the community who had issues with how they were being treated, most especially how they were treated as a result of some personal characteristic — race, gender, sexual orientation, religious affiliation. Princeton University was one of the universities that established a campus ombudsman office.

In 1993, I became the first Princeton University Ombudsman. Princeton was often referred to as the most southern-like campus in the Ivy League. There were but a handful of women and persons of color on the faculty. There were many exclusive student Dining Clubs whose memberships were strictly limited. For the most part, only the legacies were admitted to these closed enclaves. The buildings that housed these clubs, with their towering white columns, often resembled Twin Oaks, the plantation mansion in "Gone with the

114

Wind." Only recently had Princeton admitted women, so there were very few women in these clubs. And, of course, there were no black, Hispanic, or Asian members. Jews were restricted as well. Woodrow Wilson served as president of Princeton in the early twentieth century. A School of Government on the campus was named for him. He was an avowed racist. (Princeton has just recently renamed that school.) Into this environment, I stepped as the first University Ombudsman.

My learning from this experience focused not on race, so much on culture. The differences in wealth between the traditional Princeton student and the newly admitted scholars of color presented almost insurmountable barriers to understanding. For example, while students of color had rarely, if ever, ventured outside of their restricted neighborhoods, the wealthy Princeton students had traveled extensively outside of the United States. While students of color went home for the holidays, these students often went to Vail, Colorado or the Swiss Alps for skiing vacations. Here, worlds could only be bridged with committed intentionality to work and study together. The Ombudsman, along with others, was expected to help bridge this gap.

During this time, the organizational ombudsman was gaining traction in corporate America as well. McDonal-Douglass, TIAA-CREF. Coca-Cola and Chevron had ombudsman offices at this time. Having seen the value of the organizational ombudsman in other institutions in the corporate world and faced with the potential discrimination lawsuits based on race and gender, Shell Oil Company (Shell US) decided to retain an organizational ombudsman. I was fortunate to be chosen for this role and assumed the position of Corporate Ombudsman for Shell Oil (Shell US) in Houston, Texas in 1997. One of the goals of the organizational ombudsman is to prevent litigation through the use of conflict resolution mechanisms, including the ombudsman. Here, my legal experience was seen as a valuable tool to assist in this effort. While the conflicts at Princeton often centered on gaps in wealth and income, the differences at Shell often stemmed from race and gender. An oil company is primarily a culture of science and engineering, a haven for white men. Like Princeton, Shell established a goal to increase the diversity of its workforce. With more women and people of color coming into an organization that historically denied opportunities to these groups, the challenge, nevertheless, was similar to that faced by Princeton. "Now that the institution has been successful in achieving some level of diversity, how do we manage the conflict that will inevitably result?" Using my Princeton experience, I determined that a key to successful conflict resolution (this time based on gender and race), was the establishment of trust between those in conflict. While the diagnosis was somewhat easy, the establishment of trust, not between groups but between committed individuals, took an extraordinary effort.

Unlike Princeton and Shell US, the International Monetary Fund housed one of the oldest organizational ombudsman offices in the world. After World War II, the United Nations, the World Bank, and the International Monetary

Fund were established to promote world peace and stability, thereby alleviating the conditions that might lead to World War III. A mandate in the creation of these organizations would be that the leadership and the staff would reflect the people of the member countries. Never in the history of the world had so many different classes, races, cultures, and religions come together to work together. To address these inevitable conflicts, each of these organizations established its own ombudsman office early in its development.

Therefore, when I arrived at the IMF in Washington D.C. in 2005, the expectation was that I would continue the work of the ombuds who had preceded me. My experiences at Princeton and Shell Oil did not fully prepare me for the culture of the IMF. At the IMF, the differences were multi-faceted and did not conform to uni-level differences in wealth, gender, or race. Here, the landscape included all of these differences and more. There was an element of Western European/American hegemony. After all, these Euro-Americans had won the war and were now in charge. And because the funding of these organizations was based on economic viability, the West dominated. Still, the learning that I took from the IMF was not about the traditional differences. Here, the enlightenment that I experienced was about religion. I assumed my position at the IMF shortly after 9/11. While I had worked with people of different statuses of wealth, gender, and race, I had never had the opportunity to work within an environment of religious tension. And there was the Israeli-Palestinian discord. The Muslim world had been portrayed, especially at this time, as terrorists and haters. I found that Muslims in the IMF were serious believers committed to their faith, just as those of other faiths were seriously committed to their beliefs.

From these three very different cultural experiences, I took away what to me has become profound learning. We do not have to agree. While uniformity and conformity are beyond our reach, respect is within our grasp. As long as respect is our approach to others, especially with those with whom we are at odds, we can live, work, and thrive together for the flourishing of humankind.

--
WILBUR HICKS, JD is an Adjunct Professor in the School of Education and Urban Studies. His interest is in education and the law.
Email: wilbur.hicks@morgan.edu

34

I Am Not Your Black Diamond: Breaking Eleven Years of Silence

Sharlene Allen-Milton
School of Social Work

At his court hearing, the Honorable Nelson Mandela (1962) stated,

I hate the racial arrogance which decrees that the good things of life shall be retained as the exclusive right of a minority of the population, and which reduces the majority of the population to a position of subservience and inferiority and maintains them as voteless chattels to work where they are told and behave as they are told by the ruling minority. I am sustained in that hatred by the fact that the overwhelming majority of mankind both in this country and abroad are with me.

Incidences of discrimination and prejudice can have a profound impact on the psyche. This essay discusses how graduate-level cross-cultural study involving prejudice affected me and led me to change for the better.

Proud to Be Me

Growing up in the African American and Caribbean side of the Bronx of New York City as a first-generation Caribbean-American I did not experience racial discrimination. My Caribbean family members were many shades of Black and White, and so were my friends. I grew up in a community where women and men worked hard, whether in white-collar or blue-collar jobs, and African American and Caribbean culture was celebrated. When I visited my middle-class family in the Caribbean, I was surrounded by prosperous people who looked like me. I was confident and proud of being a Caribbean-American woman.

Cross Cultural Study Opportunity

I wanted to study abroad since high school but had to wait until my late 30s to do so. In 2011, during my second year as a doctoral student, an international elective course was offered entitled "Leadership in Organizations." This course involved a 5-day learning-intensive experience in Cape Town, South Africa. A month before my trip, I completed the required leadership readings and learned about South Africa (the Rainbow country), with its first democratic presidential vote electing Nelson Mandela, who used *ubuntu* ("I am because we are") to unify the country. I became familiar with South Africa's racial stratifications, plight with HIV/AIDS, and inequities, as well as its tourist attractions.

After the 14-hour flight, I arrived at a beautiful hotel, The Commodore. When Black hotel staff saw me, they thought I was rich because it was an anomaly for Black women to stay in the hotel for 5 days. It was amazing seeing women with my color and plus-sized physique star in soap operas, serve as talk show hosts, and hold prominent positions in the media. My pleasantly plump physique was viewed as beautiful! I was often mistaken for a native of the Xhosa (pronounced Kosa in English but the Xh has a clicking sound as if you are calling a horse) people, the second-largest ethnicity in South Africa. As I walked to the supermarket, which was located inside the mall, a Xhosa woman talked to me in her native dialect and was surprised when I didn't understand. She would then reply, "Excuse me, Ma; I thought you were Xhosa. My sister, you look like one of us!" This was a repetitive occurrence.

During our stay, we visited many tourist attractions such as Cape Hope (the most southern point of the African continent), the zoo, and Table Top Mountain. Another amazing experience was the Gold Restaurant. Visiting this restaurant was an immersive African experience where I engaged in a pre-dinner interactive djembe drumming session, introduced to 14 dishes representing various African countries, spices, and cooking techniques. Post-dinner entertainment included Mali life-sized puppets and songs of praise that welcomed the guests. The singing was filled with rich harmonies that touched the soul. Although I didn't understand the words, I believe there was a part of my DNA that did. To me, it felt that those songs of welcome were as if I and my ancestors who were separated from the continent because of slavery were being welcomed back home. There was a moment when I was overcome with emotion that I sobbed from a deep place.

The Lesson of the Black Diamond
The educational portion of the trip was a mixed experience. It was wonderful visiting Robbin Island and learning of Nelson Mandela, as well as visiting a global leadership class at the University of Cape Town, seeing a Black female professor, and hearing about the growing Black middle class. On the other hand, there was one experience during our lectures that I have kept silent about until now.

We met with three business consultants (two White South African men and one South African woman) to learn about the context of their operational business environment. Three graduate students participated in this learning experience: a first-generation Indian American female master's student, a White male master's student, and myself. Introductions included work experience, background in leadership, and future goals. During my introduction, I shared how I had a bachelor's degree in social work from Morgan State University and a master's degree in clinical social work from Smith College. I also shared that I had over 15 years of experience as a clinical social worker, in middle management and private practice. I closed by sharing that as a result of directing the foster care program of two offices 125 miles apart, I was interested in research on leading dispersed teams.

Through first-hand experience, we examined differences in leadership across cultures and requirements for cultural intelligence. During the second day, one of the male managers referred to my work with dispersed teams as if it were the work of the Indian American student. My professor, a White woman, repeatedly corrected him, noting that the idea was that of "Sharlene, the senior doctoral student." Despite the clarification, the manager continued with the error. It reached a point where the Indian American woman corrected him by saying, "That's not me; that's Sharlene." Although at first, this appeared to be an honest mistake, I started to think it was purposeful.

On day 2, there was a lecture on the cross-cultural implications of strategic alliances and linkages and the cultural meaning of work in organizations in South Africa. The first part focused on diversity, equity, and inclusion efforts in the country as a result of the end of apartheid (Burger & Jafta, 2010). There was a discussion regarding the country's efforts to institute affirmative action and make workplaces more equitable, increasing the numbers of Black and Indian managers. The same manager who gave the credit for my work to another student spoke about the increase of Black managers and the phenomenon of "Black Diamonds." He mentioned numerous people "losing their jobs to Black Diamonds" or Black managers who were allegedly favored into managerial positions because of Affirmative Action so companies could meet quotas for receiving government contracts. He also reported that these Black Diamonds were South Africa's new middle class and were often viewed as irresponsibly spending their money on flashy cars and flamboyant clothes. During the lecture, he commented, "Sharlene, if you were to move here, you would make a good Black."

For the rest of the lecture, time stood still. I reviewed his statement in my mind as if I were mistaken about what I heard. When we took a break, I facetiously said to my professor, "Wow, I am considered a Black Diamond in the country." My professor responded, "That was not a compliment." At the end of our time together, my professor again introduced me as the senior student and noted that I would be presenting gifts of thanks to the managers on behalf of the university, which involved shaking hands and taking pictures. I wondered if this was her passive-aggressive attempt to get back at the manager who suggested that I would make a good Black Diamond.

Processing my 2-day experience in my hotel room, I felt belittled. I felt that my above-average academic career in higher education, including my 3.75 GPA as a doctoral student, and my professional social work career were being discredited. I felt that the manager resented the positive changes in diversity, equity, and inclusion that were occurring in the country and was attempting to use me as a scapegoat—erasing me and my accomplishments from the room.

How I've Changed

This cross-cultural study abroad experiences left me with mixed feelings. On one hand, I realized that beauty is subjective. Although the standard of beauty is changing in America, for the most part, it remains that the standard of beauty is largely associated with European features, slim, straight nose, and long straight hair. This trip changed that paradigm as I along with my plus-sized physique was viewed as beautiful and accepted. On the other hand, my experience in the leadership class had a 10-year-long impact on my psyche in the form of imposter syndrome. Coined by Clance and Imes (1978), imposter syndrome is the persistent inability to believe that one's success is deserved or has been legitimately achieved because of one's own efforts or skills. In my late 30s to mid-40s, I often wondered if I was good enough or if my education, work, or aspects of my curriculum vita would be questioned as legitimate.

According to Leaf (2020), negative thoughts can be wired into the brain, and they can also be wired out. Engaging in therapeutic work and relying on my spirituality aided me in knowing that I was not a Black Diamond, as the term was pejoratively used. Through the power of affirmations, I was able to cancel the negative messaging associated with imposter syndrome. I learned that individuals' distorted perceptions and projections are not facts, nor are they reflections of my reality. I've learned the importance of a positive mindset that views challenges and obstacles as learning opportunities. Stories like this bring awareness to issues of discrimination in higher education and in cross-cultural study abroad experiences. This story also highlights ways of overcoming the stress associated with discrimination and work-life management for graduate students of color and the cathartic expression of writing.

References

Burger, R., & Jafta, R. (2010). *Affirmative action in South Africa: An empirical assessment of the impact on labour market outcomes* [CRISE Working Paper 76]. Centre for Research on Inequality, Human Security and Ethnicity.

Clance, P. R., & Imes, S. A. (1978). The imposter phenomenon in high achieving women: Dynamics and therapeutic intervention. *Psychotherapy: Theory, Research & Practice, 15*(3), 241–247.

Leaf, C. (2020). 3 Signs your body is in toxic stress and what you can do about it. https://drleaf.com/blogs/news/3-signs-your-body-is-in-toxic-stress-and-what-you-can-do-about-it

Mandela, N. (1962). Black man in a white court: Nelson Mandela's First Court Statement—1962. https://www.un.org/en/events/mandeladay/court_statement_1962.shtml

SHARLENE ALLEN-MILTON is an Assistant Professor in the School of Social Work with research interests in dispersed social work, as well as health and well-being, specifically work-life management for professional women and students of color. Email: Sharlene.allen@morgan.edu

35

Learning Language, Learning Philosophy

Seth Vannatta
Department of Philosophy

I once learned in a philosophy of education class that significant differences existed between books intended to teach young children to read in the United States and in China. My professor reminded me of our first sentences: "The cat sat on the mat." "The dog is brown." "The duck has white feathers." The sentences were observations about objects in the world, and the sentence structure was often Aristotelian in a nature where some category is predicated of a simple subject. Thus, while we were learning to pronounce words, we were also being inculcated into a worldview, one that was empirical and classificatory. The empiricist gains knowledge through observation, and then classifies it according to predicates or categories, potentially educating the young into an insider/outsider logic. The dog is a member of the category of all brown things. The duck falls outside that category. Both the process of this education and the logic learned could have far-reaching implications, I thought.

Bracketing the question as to whether such potential indoctrination into empiricism and Aristotelian logic were nefarious, I was told that in China, the earliest sentences read by young children included those such as: "Little brother respects big brother." "Brother and sister honor grandfather and grandmother." "Big sister treats little sister with kindness." These sentences not only taught students to pronounce Chinese characters. They also instructed children into a Confucian worldview including the importance of family and the values of respect, honor, and kindness. I imagined this philosophy of education would have practical consequences as well.

I traveled to Freiburg, Germany to study the German Language at the Goethe Institute during my summer vacation from teaching middle school in 2001. I did this in anticipation of going to graduate school to study philosophy and needing to pass a translation exam in one or more languages. My French and Latin were passable, but I knew no German, an important language in the study of philosophy. So, I had the chance to learn to read German the way young children read German, and I recall clearly one of the passages I read accompanied by pictures of a German man and a German police officer. The man stood on one side of a painted line, and the police officer pointed at him and said, "Das kannst du nicht tun!" (You cannot do that). The man replied, "Warum nicht?" (Why not?) And the officer answered, "Das ist verboten." (That is forbidden). My comment to my teacher was "Das ist kein Grund." (That is not a reason). She understood my protest, but I think reading that exchange taught me something about the German worldview, a respect for authority, come what may.

For example, walking on a weekend through Freiburg with a few fellow students and some German locals, we encountered a street entirely devoid of cars, scooters, or bicycles. The red-light icon indicated that it was not time to walk across the street. So no one took a step. I couldn't believe that these pedestrians would obey this inanimate light when there was clearly no danger in crossing the street in sight. Nevertheless, they waited patiently and proceeded across when the light changed, rather than when it was merely practically safe.

Four years later I traveled to Oxford, England on a fellowship to study British history and politics, as I was teaching high school British History at the time. One of my favorite memories was a trip I took by train to Scotland to watch the Open Championship, one of professional golf's most prestigious tournaments held in 2005 at the Old Course at St. Andrews and won by none other than Tiger Woods. What I witnessed on that weekend trip at the tournament was a microcosm of a very different worldview than the one I experienced in Germany. We drank tallboy beers with a professional rugby team who laughed and sang and cussed like sailors. In Britain, the people ruled.

SETH VANNATTA is Professor and Chair of the Department of Philosophy and Religious Studies at Morgan State University. He is the author of *Conservatism and Pragmatism in Law, Politics, and Ethics* (Palgrave Macmillan, 2014). His areas of interest include American Pragmatism, philosophy of law, philosophy of education, and popular culture and philosophy.
E-mail: seth.vannatta@morgan.edu

36

Intellectual and Cultural Humility: My Reflection on a Series of Moments During the Ghana Excursion

Dia Sekayi
Department of Advanced Studies, Leadership and Policy

> *"And the day came when the risk to remain tight in a bud was more painful than the*
> *risk it took to blossom."*
> *— Anais Nin*

Introduction

My most notable international experience took place in Ghana, West Africa in the year 2000. This annual three-week group study trip was organized by one of my doctoral professors. I had heard about previous trips and was excited to finally find myself in a position to travel. My reflection on the experience at the time was quite positive. The trip took place at a time in my life that was filled with the uncertainty of a professional move and physical relocation, and the joy and conflict of deep self-exploration; this was truly perfect timing. When I reflect on my international experience today, it stands as one of the most memorable experiences of my life. Today, my interpretation highlights the importance of cultural and intellectual humility for my personal and professional growth (Cobb, 2019; Hook, et al 2013).

I taught for a few years at an African-centered school in the U.S. and we spent so much time drawing parallels between African American and various west African cultures that I embarked on this journey believing that my Ghanaian brothers and sisters and I were the same, just separated by an ocean. We had engaged in some cultural instruction in preparation for travel and this included some rudimentary language instruction. I found the welcome to be warm, particularly when the effort was made to speak Twi.

I was moved by my experiences in the smaller villages. The offering of welcome water upon entry to someone's home and being 'walked down a piece of the road' as you left. These are things I experience when I visit Black folks' homes in the U.S., especially in the south. These experiences reinforce my connection with brothers and sisters on the Continent and to the land itself.

Theory and Practice

I learned and taught about the cultural context for more than a decade prior to this trip, but this was truly my first experience being embedded in an unfamiliar context for an extended visit, so this was my opportunity to practice what I had been taught and what I had been teaching.

I'd completed my doctoral program five years prior to my journey to Ghana and had just accepted a faculty position at Howard University at the Associate Professor rank, but one of the early and residual feelings from the experience is that I was not seen as a legitimate academic there. More than a few times I heard "you don't look like a lecturer". On my way to what was a transformative life experience, I was already experiencing some impostor syndrome, so being told repeatedly that I did not look the part was distracting at best and disorienting at times.

My current research examines the usefulness of intellectual humility for doctoral students. I could have used that knowledge during my time in Ghana. I believe that I am a good listener, and I am naturally intellectually curious. Even so, I was unprepared. As an African American woman, the only privilege with which I was familiar is that associated with being a cis-gendered, heterosexual individual. But as we know, one of the benefits of privilege is the freedom from having to think about being oppressed. I learned in Ghana that the American part of my identity was prioritized and privileged, but when intertwined with my identity as a woman, I felt somewhat muted. In fact, in addition to being told that I did not look the part, I was told to be silent several times over the course of my visit.

The Video

We had gathered at the home of one of our hosts. We were shown a video that was framed as a female rites of passage ceremony. As I watched, I realized that the ceremony was a circumcision, also known as female genital mutilation (O'Neill & Pallitto, 2021). My horror was evident, but I was discouraged from speaking. I was unable to apply the cultural humility to the experience in that moment that it would have taken for me to simply listen and learn. At that time in my personal development, I felt obliged to speak my mind when something incensed me. More than two decades later, I know that taking time to ruminate in facts, feelings, and interpretations has value. I believe I would have reached the same conclusion, but the content and method of my communication would

125

have been more refined and perhaps received differently. This was my first lesson in cultural and intellectual humility; there would be others.

The Bookstore

One of our activities was a visit to a bookstore. I was astounded not about the fact that there were so many Ghanaian (and other African) publications in my professional area of interest, but by the fact that I was completely unfamiliar with the authors as these works had not been available to me in the U.S., particularly at the time I was writing my dissertation. I am mindful that in the early nineties when I was engaged in my dissertation research, the internet was not the primary source for academic information. I was, however, under the impression at that time that our databases (card catalogs) included all publications even if they were not available in our library. I realize now how ridiculous that sounds, but that moment highlighted my lack of cultural and intellectual awareness. The realization that there was/is a parallel universe of scholarship may have been the genesis of the development of my intellectual humility.

The Pencil

Another pivotal moment occurred when we arrived at a small village. We had been asked to donate school supplies to the local school. On this day, some of those supplies were given to the children. I watched a young boy beam and celebrate with a dance upon receipt of a pencil. I was so overcome with emotion that I had to go back to the van to compose myself. I could only think about what it would take for a privileged, or even a not so privileged, American child to celebrate with such vigor. I thought about all the things I took for granted. This was so easy for me to do. Privileges associated with being American are mitigated by one's gender and racial identity, but they are privileges nevertheless.

Summary

Though my trip abroad took place more than two decades ago, it remains one of the most transformative experiences of my life. What I learned during my brief stay in Ghana still informs my thinking and my relationships with international students and colleagues. That trip showed me how the world is large and small at the same time. The tight bud of a life lived only in the U.S. blossomed one summer in Ghana.

References

Cobb, A. (2019). Hope for intellectual humility. *Episteme, 16*(1), 56-73. doi:10.1017/epi.2017.18

Hook, J. N., Davis, D. E., Owen, J., Worthington Jr., E. L., & Utsey, S. O. (2013). Cultural humility: Measuring openness to culturally diverse clients. *Journal of Counseling Psychology*. doi:10.1037/a0032595

O'Neill, S., & Pallitto, C. (2021). The consequences of female genital mutilation on psycho-social well-being: A systematic review of qualitative research. *Qualitative health research, 31*(9), 1738-1750.

--

DIA SEKAYI is an Associate Professor in the School of Education and Urban Studies. She teaches research courses in the Urban Educational Leadership doctoral program. Previously she was an Assistant Director for Education in the Center for the Enhancement of Teaching and Learning and faculty at the Georgia Institute of Technology. She has published books, articles, and book chapters and made local, national, and international presentations in the social foundations of education, doctoral student development, and qualitative research methods. E-mail: dia.sekayi@morgan.edu

37

Learning Beyond the Curriculum

Gonzalo Baptista
Department of World Languages and International Studies

My Personal Experience

There is a picture in which I would like to live. The image captures me cooking a *risotto* with an old man sitting by my side, looking through his blurred glasses. As trivial as it may seem, this snapshot represents one of the best moments I have had in my study abroad experiences. Memories do not fade with the years. The day this picture was taken, that man, Egi Volterrani, taught me how to achieve the creamy consistency and the *al dente* texture of rice. We laughed, we debated approaches, we contrasted methodologies, we cooked together. As often happens with study abroad experiences, the best learning moments usually take place outside the classroom.

Egi was the director of a publishing house in Italy, where I went to learn about literary translation. This was part of an internship hosted by my university's study abroad program. That internship in Italy offered me the opportunity to live in a different country, to learn a new language, and expand my professional experience, and to make a group of outstanding friends. There were of course some challenges, but all in all the benefits of the experience have outweighed the initial difficulties. So many times, I think that if I had not started that journey, I would have never followed the path on which I am today. What would have become of my younger self if I had not decided to venture out of my country to further my education?

Ironic as it may seem, small decisions shape the future in a big way. Today, I am glad I made those decisions. After that internship at the publishing house, I decided to stay in Italy, where I lived for a decade. I traveled, I learned, I loved, I enjoyed my time there. Eventually, I came to the United States as an international graduate student. Thanks to my previous experience I was able to navigate the choppy waters of U.S. higher education. I was ready to face changes and to embrace them calmly. My curiosity for living experiences in other cultures never ended, so I also spent a year in Mexico doing research, before moving to Virginia and then Maryland.

It is true that in the place one lives, one learns the skills that will be needed in a future career or project. In my case, I enriched my life in different places, most of them abroad, learning skills far from what the academic curriculum tends to include. For example, going back to that picture, Egi was an Italian translator of Maghreb and African authors, such as Sony Lab'ou Tansi, Tahar Ben Jelloun, and Wole Soyinka. In his close circle, I also came to know a rare combination of writers, film directors, painters, and opera singers. They were people with whom I had keen conversations. Thanks to him I was exposed to narratives I would have probably never connected with if I had not frequented his house in Torino, Italy. Similar appreciation goes for the long conversations that widened my standpoint, made me think outside the box, and allowed me to enjoy a diversity of contexts.

A Non-Equal Opportunity for All

As a Spanish language professor, when I survey my Black students about having a life abroad, I mainly get two types of answers, depending on their language fluency level. Those in the beginning levels tend to be reluctant to expand their lives in another cultural context. They do not seem to be very interested. In contrast, those in higher-level courses are ardent defenders of living abroad. They even have a list of countries where they plan to live in, among them Panama, Guatemala, Mexico, and Spain. It could be understood that a good portion of these students learn the language to escape the dire reality of the United States that they experience at their age. Although studying abroad is considered a life-changing experience, problems of inequity and exclusion are evidenced in low rates of participation in college study abroad programs. Uju Anya reminds us that "Black students are 6% of program participants, while they represent 13% of postsecondary enrollees. In comparison, white students, who are 56% of the overall postsecondary student population, comprise 70% of study abroad participants" (104). This underrepresentation is linked to a chain of failures in the educational system, policies, and racism in society.

In view of this lack of referents, it is worth remembering that one of "the most prominent Americans to study abroad in the nineteenth century was undoubtedly W. E. B. Du Bois" (Beck 1). In fact, during his two years of graduate study in Berlin (1892-1894), he traveled extensively throughout Europe. That was a formative period because he acquired not only the historical and empirical methodologies that he applied to his subsequent intellectual development (Barkin 79) but also a new cultural framework to understand different angles of societal practices. Part of this experience can be traced in chapter 10 of his *Autobiography*. Although Du Bois was already well prepared by the time he arrived at the University of Berlin, he attended lectures with professors who were "critical contributors to the strategy he embraced to mitigate racism in the United States" (Barkin 80). In spite of the fact that some of his writings from that period can be understood differently today, it is worth noting that the understanding of a different political, cultural environment influenced his view and writings on the Black community and gave him a set of transferable skills that he applied in his subsequent studies. Aside from the

European-style scholarly approaches, the years in Berlin clearly "changed him on an intimate and personal level" (Beck 7). As he recalled in *The Souls of the Black Folk* (2), that period was the only time in his adulthood where he did not experience discrimination for being Black. He also practiced some societal customs. It was in Germany where "he learned how to drink beer and wine" (Beck 8) and where got the style of his beard and his distinguished demeanor, including the fashion of wearing cane and gloves.

If Du Bois was a prominent international student in the nineteenth century, we can also celebrate other contemporary references that may inspire Black students to go overseas. For instance, the first National Youth Poet Laureate Amanda Gorman spent a semester in Spain, where she continued her education in Creative Writing at the Universidad Complutense de Madrid, back in 2019. While thinking about what kind of poet she wanted to be, she strengthened her Spanish language skills. She wrote new poetry in Spanish, published it in Madrid, and read it in front of an international audience—undoubtedly, in Spanish. She emphasizes that "the sky is the limit when you are studying abroad" (Gorman). She is only one recent example illustrating a successful experience while studying abroad. She may stimulate other students to continue their formation, not only in Europe, but in other countries where the legacy and stories of the Black diaspora is more present, such as Brazil, Colombia, Cuba, Mexico, Peru, or Venezuela.

Conclusions

Considering that we all relate to various identities (race, ethnicity, gender, sexual orientation, social class, among others), my personal study abroad experience helped me to navigate the multicultural and multilingual world in which we live today. I was privileged enough to have had a one-year internship in Italy, to be an international graduate student in the United States, and to have conducted academic research in Mexico. In all three places, I have understood different ways of thinking and interacting with the members of the community I lived with. The skills one gets are not only related to the curriculum but can be applied to other areas. For me, engaging culturally with culinary practices inspired me to explore the connection between food and people. My experience confirms that the courses linked to the academic curriculum are relevant. There is no question about this—but it is also true that there is a world waiting for students: a new country, possibly another language, surely new people to meet and care about, definitely a remarkable culture.

Having referents is also important to continue a path and feel safe while familiarizing oneself with a less known culture and society. Although distant in time close in pioneering, W. E. B. Du Bois and Amanda Gorman epitomize two relevant study abroad models for students today. Both already had a noteworthy aptitude to explain society, one with a sharp sociological eye, the other with a multifaceted poetic vision. For both, the experience abroad stimulated them to bring new ideas and gave them a platform to see local issues with a different appreciation.

Gonzalo Baptista cooking a risotto with Egi Volterrani. Torino, Italy, 2009.

References

Anya, U. (2020). African Americans in world language study: The forged path and future directions. *Annual Review of Applied Linguistics*, 40, 97-112.

Barkin, K D. (2000). Berlin days, 1892-1894: W. E. B. Du Bois and German political economy. *Boundary*, 27(3), 79-101. https://doi.org/10.1215/01903659-27-3-79.

Beck, H (1996). W.E.B. Du Bois as a study abroad student in Germany, 1892-1894. *Frontiers: The Interdisciplinary Journal of Study Abroad*, 2(1),45-63, https://doi.org/10.36366/frontiers.v2i1.25.

Bois, D., & Burghardt, W. E. (1961). *The souls of the Black folk : Essays and sketches.* Fawcett.

Gorman, A. (2021). *Amanda Gorman, National Youth Poet Laureate and IES Abroad Madrid Alum, on The Power of Study Abroad.* https://www.youtube.com/watch?v=aKCrqmi-55M.

Gonzalo Baptista (originally from Spain) is an Assistant Professor of Spanish and Italian at the Department of World Languages and International Studies at Morgan State University. His major research interests lie in the areas of displacement (exile, migrations, etc.), education, and the interconnections of the African diaspora in Europe. Email: gonzalo.baptista@morgan.edu

38

A Divine Encounter to Remember

Jacqueline Holland
Department of Faculty, Family and Consumer Sciences

I was excited about my trip to Mauritius. I was meeting friends there for a conference whose purpose was for spiritual and personal refreshment. Mauritius is a small African nation located in the Indian Ocean. The first leg to my final destination had me board a plane in Atlanta, Georgia, United States, en route to Paris, France. As I entered the cabin to locate my seat, the aircraft was chilly as usual, very typical for overnight international flights. I was looking forward to my window seat and nestling in for the eight-hour flight. As I approached my seat, I came upon a woman there.

Encased in an airline blanket with her eyes closed, she appeared cold. Because of the lateness of the hour and knowing there would not be much to see in the darkness, I thought to myself, "okay," no problem, she looked so comfortable tucked in under her blanket by the window. After placing my luggage in the overhead compartment, I sat in the adjacent seat. We greeted one another warmly. After some time, we engaged in conversation. She indicated that she was from Mauritius and had been in the United States for a few weeks visiting her daughter in California, who was in a graduate program there. As we continued getting to know one another, I discovered she was a classroom teacher just like me.

She was recently retired from teaching social studies and history in secondary school. I explained that I was an educator in family and consumer sciences, also known as home economics. Yasmin indicated her sister was a Home Economics (HEc) teacher; I was pleasantly surprised! In the United States, the name was changed to Family and Consumer Sciences (FCS) several years ago. At that moment, we had something in common.

After a few hours of sleep, as dawn came upon us, we continued getting to know one another. She told me about her country and some places I should visit during my stay. I enjoyed getting to know this new friend; it was effortless to talk to her. I sensed she felt the same about me. As we were nearing the destination, France, our flight times to Mauritius differed, and we exchanged contact information. She was very familiar with the hotel where I would be staying and promised to contact me while there. She indicated her family members often visited that hotel when they wanted to get away for the weekend. As the conversation ensued, Yasmin gave me her phone number to contact her if time permitted. Little did I know this brief intentional acquaintance would result in many memorable experiences.

A few days before leaving Mauritius, I gave her a call. To my surprise, Yasmin had contacted the hotel several times, though I never received her messages. I was just impressed and touched that she was a woman who kept her promise to follow up with me. She picked me up from the hotel, and we spent a day together. I had the opportunity to meet her sister, Shi when we visited Aleemiah College, where she taught. Upon entering the home economics classroom, I felt like I was back in the United States. The adolescent female students were all dressed in uniform, donned with hair covering and aprons, like my students in America. They huddled around their teacher, who demonstrated a food preparation procedure. Afterward, they went to their respective "kitchen labs" to prepare the food item. The room was abuzz with chatter, and the students looked excited as they worked together in teams to complete the task. It made me feel right at home. Another home economics teacher invited me to speak to a class of older adolescent girls to share a bit of myself and where I lived. The students were attentive, listening to my every word and what I was sharing with them. Though I did not know French or Arabic, the teacher translated. This group discussed resource management principles for the home. It was a great experience seeing the principles of home economics taught in a different part of the world. It affirmed the power of this academic discipline and how it transforms the lives of individuals, families, and communities to flourish in positive ways. What I observed was similar to what I was doing with my students in the United States. As a field of study that assists individuals to develop the art and science of living in our complex world, FCS/HEc can be found in all levels of education, business and industry, government, human services, health, and community settings. This field encompasses food science, nutrition, personal and family finance, culinary arts, hospitality, tourism, and education. Other areas include human/child development and family relations, textiles, apparel and retailing, health management, wellness, housing, interior design, and sustainability (AAFCS, 2022). This content is universal in its approach and application to a positive quality of life.

Yasmin, Shi, and I spent the rest of the day together, eating lunch and shopping. During this time, they invited me to attend wedding reception of one of their friends the next day. Both sisters and I agreed proper attire would be necessary. They took me to a small clothing shop near their home to select a garment. I will never forget the scene of selecting appropriate apparel and witnessing these two women barter with the shop owner for the price of the garment that I would end up purchasing. I felt very well cared for with these two sisters and was astonished by how they embraced me. The garment needed a small alternation, and Yasmin completed it artfully! Shi provided the shoes.

The reception was a wonderful occasion of celebrating a marriage through food, song, dance, and fellowship through a culture different from my own. While visiting Yasmin's home, we virtually spoke with each other's families. It was good meeting them, and she enjoyed meeting my family. On our last day together, we spent it at the beach. Yasmin and I have maintained our friendship and connected remotely consistently though our time difference is 11 hours. This divine encounter enriched my life. Taking the opportunity to open to others and getting to know them can be associated with discovering a goldmine. Seeking to understand another and respecting their way of life is an investment that reaps dividends. The value of international experiences is significant as I reflect on the numerous global journeys that I have participated in. Regardless of where our home is or the culture we embrace, humans are the same. Being open to discovering the treasure and uniqueness of another is precious.

Reference
American Association of Family and Consumer Sciences (2022). What is FCS? https://www.aafcs.org/about/about-us/what-is-fcs

---

JACQUELINE M. HOLLAND (originally from the US) is an Associate Professor and Chair in the Department of Family and Consumer Sciences. Her major research interests include housing and healthy home environments.

39

Diversifying the Colonized Mind in the Warmth of an HBCU

Denise Jarrett
Department of English and Language Arts

"Why are you beating the bottles?"

"I am teaching them, and they are not learning!"

I shouted in response to my brother who had just returned from boarding school for his summer break. He was my idol, so when I got out of my draconian mood, I greeted him with a ridiculous grin and ran into his arms. Although he was almost 14 years older, he always took the time to have a conversation with me before he greeted everyone else. My brother was the one who recreated this vista of my first teaching experience when I was leaving my seaside town, Ocho Rios to go to college in Kingston, the capital city of Jamaica to start my professional teaching career. He resuscitated the "re-memory" of my first teaching experience that was fading as he assured me that I would do well as I was indeed "cut out to be a teacher." The dramaturgical three-year-old determined to teach those bottles placed in rows like children sitting in a traditional classroom set the stage and fueled my passion to become an agent of change in a classroom at a global level.

The world became a village, and my colonial education became dense as I learned to Google and navigate the huge desktop computer which was later given the name, "The Fridge," at Excelsior Community College and High School in Kingston where I was teaching for over ten years. The change was coming. I was somewhat mastering Google, and I realized that without being reeducated, I would be left behind as there was a technology apocalypse that would limit my old skillset and render me useless. All I knew was that my sister was living in Baltimore, Maryland, so I Googled "University and Maryland" in a Boolean search. I was excited to use the new techniques that I learned in my first computer course. Obviously, the University of Maryland appeared on the screen first. I was excited, so I just applied.

I had a US visitor's visa, so as I got my summer break, I traveled to Maryland to finalize my college application. I gently broke the good news to my sister that I had applied to the University of Maryland, and I needed her to take me there to give in some papers and collect my I-20. While she endorsed my quest for further studies, she chided me in Jamaican Creole, "so what bout Morgan. Dat too far and expensive?" I knew where Morgan was. It was fifteen minutes away from my sister's house but based on my newfound love for Google and my fancy for my new computer skills, I did not remember "Dear Morgan." Thus, my Morgan journey began over twenty years ago as she did not hesitate to drive her 2000 Toyota van to the famous Montebello building.

Admissions were empty. Then he appeared. "I am Mr. Troy Quinn, the director," he said. His joviality caused me to chuckle as this thin, tall African American greeted me with exuberance. I followed his lead and returned his breeziness with a polite greeting and introduction even ending with audacity and verboseness; "please help me oh ye mighty Quinn!" juxtaposing him to the star of the 1989 movie *The Mighty Quinn*. I was jubilant when Morgan State University became my home.

While I had visited the US several times before, I was still unaware of the myriad cultures that can grow in one institution. I had professors and met students from the seven original continents and even Zealandia, earth's hidden continent since my student days and now as a tenure track assistant professor. From the time I entered Morgan, I was drawn to the diversity of cultures in this Historically Black College and University. In my homeland Jamaica, college students were usually depicted as heterosexual, upper-class, and a few middle-class people from the Caribbean along with a few scattered cultural groups from mainly Europe and Asia and a tiny sprinkle from Africa.

Many Jamaicans are guilty of being politically incorrect as they refer to all Asians as Chinese or East Indians as Coolie (a paradoxical term that is both derogatory and endearing). Additionally, there is no regard for any cultural or ethnic differences, unfortunately, an ignorant legacy from the colonizers who disrespected all other cultures. Furthermore, if you are associated with the LGBTQ+ movement, even the criminals in Jamaica will summon the Biblical "fire and brimstone" to burn out the LGBTQ+ sin, and sometimes the literal burning takes place with a gunshot or a cutlass or any other weapon.

The change from my sunny tropical island to land with four seasons symbolizes the collective changes that I had to make and practice as an educator at Morgan. One semester, a note from a female student read, "Hey Professor Jarrett, I am unable to attend class cause my girl coming today. We have not seen each other in months, so we have to be together all day and night because she going back in the morning. Do you know any Jamaican spot where we could eat? My girl likes oxtails. Do you cook them? Maybe we could come and check you out when you cooking!" A note like this to a professor in Jamaica would make the national newspapers, but these notes are commonplace in Morgan's diverse setting. I have realized that the focus for me as an English professor is to prepare my students to be excellent communicators, especially in writing. Thus, my response addressed the tone, formal and informal language, letter writing, and appropriate information along with grammar and mechanics. With this approach, the student was taught how to address someone formally and appropriately. I ignored her personal information and educated her using my position as her English professor. I had to break the aggressive teaching tool that the colonizers left, and I received on the island as I accepted all aspects of diversity.

The term "cultural awareness" is not new to any Jamaican, but from childhood, we were never taught to embrace or accept other cultures as if we are still resisting our enslavers' breaking. I developed a love for diverse cultures, and Morgan has given me the garden to interact with and understand a variety of cultures. One semester, a young man was in my class. He was always early, but he sat at the back of the room. I thought for days how to engage him. Then I realized that we liked something in common, the sport cricket. I decided to engage him because he never spoke in the class although I had fifteen other Middle Easterners who sat at the front of the class and participated. I confidently called out, "The young man at the back from Saudi Arabia, please tell the class about cricket." He did not even look at me. I looked up his name and added a little more seriousness to my tone and called his name; he then looked up. I did the unmentionable. I said, "Tell me about your Saudi Arabian Cricket team?" His face became flushed; there was total silence as he got up angrily, and shouted, "I am from Iran! I am not one of them!" I apologized profusely.

From then on, I never called a Japanese person a Chinese or a Korean either Japanese or Chinese. If I do not know the ethnic groups based on their names, I will ask. Moreover, I will never place a Muslim woman in a group with all men or students from countries that are not in good relationships together. I have also developed a thirst for the Motherland, Africa, and other places based on discussions about different customs, foods, languages, and recreational habits. Over the years, I have taken a multicultural approach when I teach English Composition 1. I have five modules consisting of topics on multicultural foods, languages, dress, religions, beliefs, sports, and other topics which I rotate every semester. Students are asked to do several projects like interviewing family members and/or international faculty, staff, or students to find out their traditional beliefs, foods, and other aspects based on their culture. The interviews are played in class, and the outcome is highly informative. Potlucks are interesting when students take in samples of cultural dishes which they share and when they wear traditional clothing. The students are then sensitized to unfamiliar cultures.

The three-year-old girl that was beating bottles to learn has flown away from punishment as a learning method to accept diversity as a teaching and social tool. I will never be a slave master and enslave my students. In fact, my goal is to free them as I have been liberated through hands-on knowledge and journeys around the world either vicariously or in reality. There are so many resources available today that can stimulate students' minds. Unfortunately, the enlightenment Morgan offers is not in all universities, but I have realized that I must accept my diverse students as I am also one flower in the diverse garden called Morgan.

DENISE M. JARRETT, Ph.D. is an assistant professor, specializing in Caribbean Literature in the Department of English and Language Arts at Morgan State University, Baltimore, Maryland. Dr. Jarrett has a special interest in Caribbean Literature, Postcolonial Literature, Ethnic and Cultural Studies, Black Cultural Productions, and Adolescence Literature. Mainly using postcolonial readings, her scholarship publications include several encyclopedia biographies and commentaries on notable African American men and women, a foreword for Canute Lawrence's 2021 poetry publication, and multiple journal articles and book chapters on Caribbean authors' works, including Michael Anthony, C. Everard Palmer, Michelle Cliff, Jamaica Kincaid, Kai Miller, Claude McKay, Vidiadhar Surajprasad Naipaul, Derek Walcott, and Shani Mootoo and African American, Toni Morrison. Dr. Jarrett also is a reviewer on Postcolonial and Ethnic and Cultural Studies for CHOICE, a stalwart book review organization connected to the Library of Congress. She also has an extensive record as chair and presenter at several national and international conferences, including West Indian Literature, Children's Literature, College Language Association, Howard University, Benjamin Quarles Symposium, and Mid-Atlantic Popular & American Culture Association Conferences, on diverse Caribbean writers, themes, and theories.

40

Not in My Classroom

Kimberly O. McManus
Department of Advanced Studies, Leadership and Policy

Everyone has a defining moment in his/her life. Some are memorable simply because of the enlightening experience that was so incredible until it would be a seeming death of a thing to let it go. On the other side of the spectrum, however, are those defining moments that exist because of the bitter taste that they leave in our mouths to encourage us to remember their staleness, and from that putrid aftertaste, we learn how to make lemons into lemonade. That is what happened in my case.

I was five years old, a happy-go-lucky kid who loved to play in the red clay of South Carolina. Being the youngest in my family, I was the last to enter school. My siblings are twins, so they had each other as they meandered the journey into education. However, it was now my turn, and I remember being nervous about going to school. I knew that my mom and dad had given me a good foundation. I was a quick learner and did very well on tests that I was given later in my kindergarten year, so much so that the school wanted to skip me two grades. So, learning was not the issue; it was meeting new people. Regardless of how well my parents had taught me to be respectful and to listen to my elders, it did not matter. Thus, I soon came to understand that my kindergarten teacher did not like me because of the color of my skin. She did not mind talking about us, African American children, as if our age made us not understand that she treated us differently than the white children in the room.

Because I was smart, she did not like me even more. She went out of her way to make me cry and have miserable days when I should have been enjoying learning how to tie my shoes to meeting new kids who were just as excited as I was to be in a room that was overwhelming with building blocks and bright wallpaper and a huge chalkboard in the middle of the room. Although I was a respectful student who raised her hand quietly waiting my turn to show my understanding of the topic, Ms. Carolyn would show her objection to my knowledge by turning her head, rolling her eyes, and making me feel that my answers were unacceptable, although correct and that my presence in her class was one that she would have wished to have avoided had she been given the opportunity.

My saving grace, however, was Ms. Judy, who was Ms. Carolyn's teacher's assistant. Ms. Judy taught me that not all white people disliked little black children who were smart because Ms. Judy, who was older, was also white, but she was always helpful and nice even when Ms. Carolyn's obvious position was to promote low self-esteem in the children who did not have blue eyes and blonde hair. For example, during picture day, Ms. Carolyn blatantly refused to help the 'black ones' because she did not want to touch our hair. At five years old, I would look at myself in the mirror and wonder if there were something wrong with me.

I remember going home and asking my mom what the difference was between one of my white friends and me. My mom told me that it was only our outward appearance because when we are cut, we all bleed the same color. In my five-year-old mind, that made a lot of sense, so with my mom telling me this, I just could not understand why Ms. Carolyn then thought it was her duty to mistreat children, nearly babies, who were coming to her for information and guidance—who looked to her for security and love even while away from home—only to shun them. It was then, at five years old, that I decided that I would teach. Looking back, I guess one would say I had an epiphany as I promised myself that I would treat all my students the same. I would not treat my students differently because they had a different color of skin or hair texture than mine.

Consequently, I started practicing being an effective teacher. To my mom's dismay, I would bring home extra copies of worksheets and sit my toys around my bedroom, pretending they were students in my class. I had a chalkboard that I used to further my teaching instruction. I was sure to call on the brown teddy bear to the white baby doll; each one had an opportunity to give an answer in my class. I promised myself that I was going to be a teacher and a darn good one!

As the years passed by, I went to Clemson and majored in Special Education. I ended up teaching students with various disabilities. Since finishing undergraduate and graduate school, I have taught on the K-12 level, the penal system, and the 2-year and 4-year levels, including master-level students. Each time I step into the classroom, I am sure to make everyone feel comfortable because I want all my students, regardless of their race, their native language, their religion, their background, their sexuality . . . to feel that they are welcomed in my class to learn. I want them to all know that I care about them because we are all in this race together.

One prime example of my maintaining my focus has been teaching students on the community college level here in Maryland. I have a pluralistic classroom, where at any given moment there are students from Africa, South America, Europe, Asia, and India. As English as a Second Language is their introduction to the post-secondary system here in the United States, I have often been many of their first American professors. They are usually very shy-acting, some afraid, of what to expect. They are not used to talking in class as it is seen as a sign of disrespect. However, I realize that when students are free to engage and discuss the learning topics, they are more likely to learn the material and apply it at a faster rate. Consequently, by the third class, students are working in groups and helping each other to learn the material.

Over the years, I have had students tell me that because I cared for each one of them as individuals and saw the potential in each of them, they were able to successfully complete their ESOL program, succeed in their other classes, and go on to have thriving careers. One student in particular, Bruno, had English as his second language and had a severe learning disability in reading and writing. However, after working with him and helping him to realize that he was just as great as the next student, he began to soar. He ended up completing a two-year associate's degree, a bachelor's, and a master's from the University of Maryland. He now gives back to his community by helping others to succeed in finding their path.

Through it all, I thank Ms. Carolyn for showing me what not to do because I could have allowed her to sour my view of education, but I did not. I could have allowed her disposition towards me to ruin my view of education, but I did not. Instead, it challenged me. I graduated valedictorian of my high school class and five degrees later, with two masters and two doctorates, I am still here . . . still loving education . . . and still passing my desire to teach and learn to new classes of students, either in my capacity as a professor or as an administrator. You know someone told me once that if life serves you lemons, make lemonade. So, I take my lemonade stand with me every day!

In hindsight, Ms. Carolyn taught me how to be resilient and how to persevere even when there is seemingly opposition standing directly in front of me. I am no longer five years old, but I am thankful for that five-year-old spirit that still lives in me, letting me know that all people deserve the right to learn and be in a welcoming environment in which to flourish and grow. Sometimes life lessons come early in life, and my discrimination lesson came early, but it taught me the person—the faculty member and administrator—that I did not want to be, and it propelled me into the person that I am. I say, therefore, *"Welcome students from every nation, from every tongue, from every belief, for the classroom belongs to you. Welcome!"*

--

KIMBERLY O. MCMANUS, Ed.D., D.Min., is a lecturer at Morgan State University in the Community College Leadership Program. Her major research interests lie in students with disabilities, first-generation students, English as a Second Language students, pastoral counseling and coaching, and minority male students. Email: kimberly.mcmanus@morgan.edu

41

Better Together: Team Teaching Across Cultures in the Age of Uncertainty

E. Blaise DePaolo
Department of Fine and Performing Arts

Susan J. Langford
Falmouth School of Arts

Only science fiction could have predicted some of the changes of the last twenty months. Like Dorothy in the *Wizard of Oz*, life, and work as we knew it was swept away into a virtual, online *Matrix* for which there was no real precedent. We had to build the plane and fly it too. The pandemic that has disrupted and taken so much has also delivered us into a virtual world of infinite possibilities on so many levels but especially when it comes to global connectedness in the university. Learning to embrace technology has been a journey from resistance and frustration to enthusiastic surrender (it does continue to be frustrating because you can never know enough and there seem to be infinite variables). Living and teaching through a pandemic have put our electronic skills acquisition on 'warp drive'. Without it, we may not have come to this collaboration as quickly as we did.

We are Dr. Sue Langford, Academic Partnership Manager, School of Entrepreneurship, Falmouth University Cornwall, UK, and Blaise DePaolo MFA, Associate Professor of Sculpture, Morgan State University, Baltimore, Maryland, USA. Our background has everything to do with why we chose to team-teach a virtual international exchange and bring Morgan service-learning students and Falmouth social action students together. We met working at Baltimore Clayworks in the late 90s. Sue in development and Blaise in programming. Clayworks is a nonprofit ceramic arts center, nationally and internationally recognized for its excellence in the field of ceramic arts, education, and community outreach. Non-profits tend to bring together teams of people who are driven by shared values and a belief in democratic principles of service and accountability.

When the pandemic forced the study, abroad model, to pivot into online virtual experiences a whole new realm of possibilities opened up for student interaction across borders. Without the expense of travel, and with state-of-the-art video conferencing, Morgan State University, an HBCU (Historically Black

143

College or University), and Falmouth University, a TWI (Traditionally White Institution) students came together during the summer of 2021 to work in teams on social justice issues. These two diverse groups came together in teams to develop either a social enterprise proposal or a public service announcement. Thanks to incredibly good professional development in virtual international exchanges and the desire to give our students a unique learning experience we teamed up again. Six months of planning and work went into our courses, countless video conferences, training sessions, and a great deal of outreach to professionals in diverse fields. There were many great moments, some awkward 'unmute yourself' moments but it was mostly very successful in delivering a teaching and learning experience like no other any of us had ever had.

Virtual exchange collaborations involve sustained collaboration among students from different cultural contexts: "are technology-facilitated, at a distance; can incorporate both synchronous and asynchronous components; are implemented in an already existing course; are carefully designed by the two (or more) professors involved typically consist of one or more shared assignments/projects/modules, occasionally; and stretching to an entire co-taught course" (DePaul University).

Morgan State students were in a summer 'mini-mester', a four-week three-credit intensive, that fulfilled one of their humanities electives. The course was explained this way:

'Community Art Virtual Exchange is a service-learning course focused on experiential education and addressing social justice issues in society. Summer Session I, 2021, GENL396 students will be tasked with working as a member of a team to develop an advertising campaign and PSA (public service announcement) aimed at addressing a social justice need such as; promoting environmentally sustainable practices as part of the Morgan State University culture. Using this example, you will work as a group to co-develop an advertising and branding campaign, educating the Morgan community on how to recycle and minimize single-use plastic. Using both creative and leadership skills, demonstrated in the social enterprise business model, students will create a body of work that can inform Morgan's future in meaningful ways. Students will either use the sustainable campus concept described above or propose another similar and mutually agreed upon the concept for a socially engaged advertising campaign. Dr. Langford's course (Falmouth BUS388) and Professor DePaolo's course (Morgan GENL 396) have intersecting content. Our virtual team-teaching approach across cultures will encourage new ways of understanding national social justice issues as global social justice issues. Additionally, students will gain valuable cultural competencies by interacting with their peers in the United Kingdom.'

The Falmouth students were on a condensed two-year BA(Hons) in Entrepreneurship, this was their final module. It was designed to build on their previous two years of study and enable them to 'do something for real' before they graduated. A module description follows:

In this module, you will be tasked with developing a social enterprise concept in response to a 'wicked problem' posed at the start of the module. You will work in groups to co-develop and validate the concept proposed. In doing so, you will consider the challenges of the Fourth Industrial Revolution and a range of societal challenges.

For example, you will:
Engage with Design Thinking as a promising theoretical framework
Critically evaluate the claims of its proponents and consider its limitations
Consider how practitioners apply the theory in a practical context, assessing how useful it can be in solving problems in our own contexts.

You'll be expected to produce and share research on relevant audiences and markets, toward developing feasible (as well as innovative) solutions. You'll be expected to use collaborative tools, synchronous and asynchronous, to work with your team on a regular basis. You will be expected to 'do something for real', either working for an established CIC, charity or non-profit or work towards establishing your own.

Your assessment will be a critical journal (60%) and presentation (40%). The journal will include research, an overview, and justification of your group's method and approach, project outcomes, group roles, etc. You will be assessed not on the outcomes of the project in terms of 'success', but rather on your critical reflection on and responsiveness to challenges, and on the dedicated application of your skillset to the given challenge.

There were many obstacles to overcome in the planning of this exchange and not all our conditions were perfect. At any given point along the six-month journey of planning, we could have given up because the circumstances weren't ideal, or the technology was daunting, but we cheered each other on. We didn't have a shared platform for video conferencing and that was occasionally problematic. Ideally, we would have had a more even number of students but given the different school calendars, we had far fewer Morgan students in the summer session than we would have during fall or spring. In highlight, we should have used breakout rooms much more than we did. Having said that, the student's reaction to the course was overwhelmingly positive and the work they produced was impressive and inspiring. The following is some of their feedback:

- The collaboration element of the class is eye-opening and beneficial not just in the classroom but to life. The information shared, gained and found is uniquely connected through the class - something which cannot be artificially replicated.
- Lots of interesting guest speakers
- Inspiring insights from inspiring individuals on amazing projects that have certainly given direction toward my own project.
- You won't find this type of international virtual exchange anywhere else that combines social initiatives with multinational opinions.
- The interaction with international students and the excellent guest speakers is something you cannot get without taking part in something like this.
- Really enjoyed learning the differences in the education system and learning about the contrasting and similar challenges that they face.
- I learnt the importance of collaboration and hearing the contrast of social issues in both the US and the UK

It appears that life as we knew it will never be the same. Life inside The Matrix is the new normal. Maybe it needed to change for the benefit of the evolving nature of teaching and learning. This collaboration was the beginning of a new way to think about what the boundaries of the classroom are and what experiences are possible in both real-time and virtually.

From top left, Blaise DePaolo, Sue Langford and guest presenter Sharon Goldsmith Esq.

E. BLAISE DEPAOLO (originally from the US) received her Master of Fine Arts degree from the Rochester Institute of Technology, School of American Craft. DePaolo's travels to Mexico and Guatemala, touring Mayan ruin sites, have been a defining influence on her work. She has exhibited nationally, is a member artist at Baltimore Clayworks, and has artwork in numerous private collections. DePaolo is also a community artist, she has designed and delivered programs for diverse populations throughout Baltimore and the State of Maryland.

SUE LANGFORD (originally from the UK) is a lecturer and Academic Partnership Manager at Falmouth University, UK. She has worked at various universities including Johns Hopkins University in the USA. Her research focus is leadership, wellbeing, and career sustainability. She is an Associate Fellow of the Higher Education Academy and has recently become a trustee for a CIC. Email: sue.langford@falmouth.ac.uk

42

Kabwalala!
the Bantu Word that Saved
and Changed My Life

Anita Pandey
Department of English and Language Arts

> *. . Anything, no matter what, to get rid of thinking!*
> – Frederick Douglass

"Kabwalala!" screamed my mother in the dead of the night. I couldn't have been more than five, but I'll never forget that blood-curdling cry that my mother let out that night. I woke up drenched in sweat. I was petrified. All I could see was darkness. All I could feel was fear. I couldn't sit, stand, or lie down. I just wanted to be with my mother and to know that she was fine. Scary shadows ran up and down the bedroom wall across from the bunker bed on which I lay. I jumped down and my head hit the floor but the pain in my mother's voice numbed all else. I reached for the light switch, but it didn't work. I tried to read the darkness about me. I began to see some grey and, out of the darkness, familiar spaces appeared. I found myself making my way into my parent's bedroom. From the doorway, I could see them crouched by the bedroom window and, through the tall lilac curtains that had a grayish hue, I spotted the outlines of military-garbed men with guns drawn. Their guns were pointed at the window—at us! I tried to warn my parents, but no sounds came out of my mouth. "I also have a gun! I'm coming there!" my father shouted. I heard my mother whisper to my father in Hindi "Bahar jin ja, re!! Mardalenge!" (Listen, don't go out! They'll kill you/us!) Then, suddenly, she blurted the word "Kabwalala!" This key word and accusation in Bemba, one of the local languages of Zambia where we were stationed at the time and where I was born worked like magic. "Eh?" responded one of these soldiers as he stuck his face onto the glass and peered through, but the darkness clearly hid us from his view. I heard him arguing in Bemba. He turned to the taller shadow and yelled something that meant "You told me foreigners lived here, eh!! Wasting our time!" Disgruntled, he then beckoned to the others, and they scurried to the driveway, jumped into a car and sped away. They left our Fiat running and parked precariously on top

of planks that they had placed to slide it across the ditch that separated the main road from our house.

It would take me a few years to understand why they left so suddenly and why they left us unharmed right after my mother referred to them using a single word *kabwalala*. To my knowledge, *kabwalala* refers to the lowest or the worst of thieves, one that steals from his own family or people. While no exact equivalent for this term exists in English, anyone from a communal culture will have a relatively easy time understanding why stealing from one's own is the ultimate offense, both disgraceful and a no-no.

I still find it hard to believe that this single word saved us! We left Zambia the following month because, that week alone, at least four international residents in our neighborhood were gunned down by militia who were fighting for independence in neighboring northern Rhodesia. They would accost and rob expatriates to pay for arms and other expenses. After we left, the new expatriate residents in the home we occupied for nine years were also visited by the militia. This time, the family hid in the bathtub in the bathroom in which my father had installed multiple bolts, so a single bullet hole was insufficient to break the door. Once again, the militia leader in charge of this operation left behind a massive thumb print, and the local police department shared that he was on their "most wanted" list. He had killed a number of people that month.

I learned a valuable lesson that day; namely, that understanding the primary language in use in a locality or—speaking a smattering of it, as in this case-- even a single word could save you--literally and figuratively!

After this near-death encounter, I began to pay closer attention to my surroundings, and to keep an ear and eye out for how people communicate— the best mirror of human behavior, in my view. Immersed in a multilingual milieu, long before I started school, I learned that many cultural concepts in one language do not have equivalent structures in others. These *language building blocks*, as I term them include words, idioms, sayings, phrases, full-blown sentences, and communicative chunks beyond what we call "sentences." This realization fascinated me and is the reason I chose to study linguistics as an undergraduate student in Nigeria, and in graduate school in the United States.

I learned that night in Luanshya, Zambia that every language is a cultural vault, unique, powerful and to be treasured. In my experience, understanding and appreciating a person starts with celebrating their language(s). I understood early on that the language we employ in a specific setting sets the tone for rapport-building and trust or distrust; and it almost always determines how we are perceived, characterized, and/or viewed by those that do not know us. The language we use has the power to pacify, antagonize or even enrage the listener/reader/viewer. A basic understanding of key concepts and words, and/or other culturally significant terms in the local languages in use in a setting is, therefore, not only beneficial but highly advisable. Achieving "linguistic consonance," as I term this phenomenon of cultural adjustment that's reflected in one's choice of language can make day-to-day living very meaningful, and not merely an act of survival. This "local language power" is evident in the reaction our use of a local language almost always elicits in the listener or reader. Using a single word or a familiar sound from someone's language could bring a smile to their face! Language pride and cultural pride are synonymous for most people. I recall how a taxi driver in Canada refused to charge me all because in his words "You made me feel at home when you spoke my language! After all these years, I feel happy again!" A Nigerian woman named Hasana whom I met at the ACEI conference in Vancouver was so surprised when I greeted her with "lafiya kalau" that she immediately excused herself to purchase a pricey gift for me. What had I done to earn this gift?" I asked. "You spoke my lamnguage" she smiled. The artistic mother and child sculpture for which she paid $45 (I know because I passed the table from which she purchased it) still adorns my office desk. Her gesture made me realize how incredibly grateful and honored she was that I not merely acknowledged but celebrated her cultural heritage.

Therefore, to be a global citizen or cross-culturally aware, we must make the effort to learn or, at the very least, to understand another language or language variety. For this reason, I urge you to "learn to say hello and thank you in as many languages as possible. When greeting and expressing gratitude, you communicate that you truly care about someone. That's because each language mirrors key and unique cultural beliefs, and this explains why word-for-word translation is nearly impossible.

Through my experiences abroad, I also got to hear the musical sounds of so many more languages than if we hadn't been there, and their names intrigued and excited me: Hausa, Fulani, Igbo, Pulaar/Fulani/Fulfulde, Edo, Ijaw, ... Bhojpuri, Gujarati, Marathi, Sindhi, . . . I could go on and on! I'm certain that this exposure to different sounds, tones, stress patterns, pitch, and intonation levels has stretched my brain to new heights—beyond the kola, cumin, sumac, and the tiny, yet bold and lethal crimson "aro gete" peppers and other spices I got to smell, feel, touch, inhale, and taste. I am convinced that they have fortified my memory, my vocabulary, my disaster preparation skills, and my interpersonal communication.

I now know that cultural sensitivity is an essential interpersonal and team-building skill, and that heightened language awareness helps us to become culturally sensitive and diplomatic. Given that messages—even in one and the same language--are not always interpreted as intended, we would do well to pay close attention to how people use not just spoken language but nonverbal language, as well. When traffic suddenly came to a standstill in Ipoti, a small town in southwest Nigeria, and two drivers got into a fistfight in the middle of the road, the reason was that one driver had raised an open palm at the other driver. I saw and heard most of the bystanders amplifying and applauding the fury of the recipient of this insult. In the eyes of the community, his anger and his invitation to a fight were justified because this gesture was a brazen insult to his mother and is similar to the message you would communicate if you were furious and insolent enough to give someone the finger.

I realized that communication is a whole-body experience for many, even in America. In the most oral cultures in which we resided, most spoke with their eyes, mouths, and their limbs. They were "loud" and proud to be loud and heard. And why not? Why communicate if you are not heard or don't wish to be heard.

In my experience, developing an ear for culturally significant sounds and embracing differences in accent is another benefit of traveling and living abroad, and is, in fact, one of the first steps in becoming cross-culturally sensitive. Blowing your nose into a tissue or napkin in a public space is, for instance, considered rude in many places in which we lived. That's very likely because of the images this offensive sound conjures up in our minds. Beckoning to someone using their name is also impolite in Nigeria. Most Nigerians would rather use the snake-like hissing sound "ssssss" to call out to someone. Why? Not only because this sound reverberates and therefore carries far, but because uttering one's name out loud is generally considered disrespectful. "You reduce the power of their name when you call out to someone after they have left" is the rationale offered to me by a classmate. "It's better to call them using this sound!" she advised as she began to demonstrate.

Have you ever been hesitant to make a purchase or work with someone because of their accent? Some people are put off by what they describe as a "thick accent." The reality is that everyone who speaks a language has an accent. An accent is simply the sound quality of one's speech and a mark of our identity. The way we pronounce words; the stress and intonation patterns that we employ; and the pitch and tone of our voice, collectively yield our "accent." Some of us have a regionally distinct accent, such as a New York accent or what is broadly described as a "northern accent," while others have an accent that signals their ties to a specific social class or ethnic group. Our understanding of messages can sometimes be compromised by noise (physical, psychological, and semantic), and an unfamiliar accent is sometimes construed as one such barrier. Has it ever occurred to you that you might be the one that is hard to understand, and not the other way around? That's what I realized when we moved from country to country in the first 12 years of my life. I understood early on that I must not only develop a tolerance for differences in accent, but I must pay closer attention to the content as opposed to the sounds through which it is articulated.

In my Business and Technical Writing courses, I have shared with my students how in the heyday of outsourcing, many U.S. companies based in India prioritized and provided accent neutralization training in a bid to eliminate their Indian employees' accents. However, this practice of minimizing and/or obliterating one's heritage accent is exclusionary and contrary to the professional mantra of cultural acceptance and inclusion. As I remind my students before you decide to drop a class because you have trouble decoding your instructor's accent, make sure to give yourself some time to get accustomed to the stress pattern(s), tone, pitch, and intonation your instructor or TA employs. The longer you listen and the closer the attention you pay, the easier decoding and communication generally become. In short, patience, an open mind, and sustained contact can help to minimize and eliminate accents and many other communication barriers.

By rephrasing and by seeking clarification (i.e., whenever the task of decoding an accent became challenging), I found it so much easier to communicate and to encourage my listener to speak more freely and sans embarrassment or fear or compunction. In different parts of Africa, I actually found myself mimicking the accents in which I was addressed, and this almost always made me come across as a Nigerian, as opposed to an outsider. I watched how my father, as dark-skinned as he is, went from being called "oyinbo" (a white man or outsider) and "bature" (in Hausa) to being considered a fellow Nigerian or "one of us" almost as soon as he addressed street vendors in one of the many indigenous languages. The prices dropped just as quickly, and smiles and laughter made the haggling and market exchanges more interactive and exciting. When visitors to Nigeria made the effort to speak a Nigerian language or even pidgin or "Broken English," I saw and heard how effusively they were applauded. Their language use communicated a localized, culturally appreciative, and shared experience, so they were no longer considered outsiders, and, believe me, word got around!

Speaking of words, as cliché as this might sound, here's a word to the wise: the word is not the most important piece of language in every part of the world, and word usage and word content or meaning vary from place to place, language to language, and even within a single language! Remember this the next time someone attempts to have a word with you! The word "stranger" for instance, refers to visitors (or friends) in Nigeria. The local term for outsiders coincides with the word for colonist or "white man" in most indigenous languages. For this reason, after spending 12 years in Nigeria, the American concept of "stranger danger" initially sounded strange to me. Even though English is the global lingua franca or link language, I began to recognize and appreciate subtle and stark differences in word usage. Many words, for instance, are non-translatable because they encode unique cultural ideas or concepts. Examples include the term "slim thick," a positive way of referring to a full-figured woman in Black English Vernacular, and "najar or nazar" in Hindi and Urdu, respectively. The latter is equivalent to what in Arabic is termed "hased," the concept of the evil eye. Exposure to such expanded vocabulary—within and across languages—is essential to our personal growth and development, as well as for enhanced interpersonal and communication skills. Do I have any final words on this aspect of my language discovery, or could foraging further into lexical differences make this piece hard to digest or wordy?

I also discovered early on through my onsite experiences that language serves different functions in different cultural and geographic settings. Indeed, it does! The purposes for which we employ language, and the way we organize our thoughts, in both speech and writing, differ. While most of us use language to convey certain shared functions, such as informing, persuading/selling, and requesting, some individuals use language to communicate culturally distinct functions. Complimenting a father on his daughter's beauty, for example, is a distinct communicative function that is conveyed in Yoruba through the phrase "iyawo mi," meaning "my wife." So, when my older sister, then 16, was addressed as "my wife" by a male visitor to our home, my father was angry at first until he was informed that the term was simply intended as a compliment.

I realized through my cultural immersion that languages tend to be more interactive in oral cultures. How so? In Nigeria, for instance, the Nigerian English phrase "well done!" is frequently employed by bystanders to publicly acknowledge and celebrate a feat or a community uplifting task. In contrast, in America, "well done" is typically used in connection with steak and other meats. With the exception of neighbors, acquaintances and friends, other observers rarely show appreciation for the efforts demonstrated by community members who wash their cars, cut their grass, and so on. Food consumption is also a visibly shared and interactive experience in many communal cultures. How so? First, before food is consumed in public spaces, it is typically offered to anyone seated or standing in the vicinity. Most bystanders will decline the offer, yet to eat without offering other witnesses to this act of consumption is considered rude. Additionally, in most of the languages spoken, reference is made to eating as those who are eating are frequently told to enjoy their meals. This function is akin to "buen provecho" and "bonne appetite" in Spanish and French respectively.

The function of showing respect, beyond the general terms "Sir" and "Ma'am," is another example. In Nigeria and India, for example, I saw how this culturally significant communicative function was realized through the use of honorifics like -ji appended at the end of names (e.g., Anita-ji!) and through the use of additional signals of respect like "Sir" and "Madam," and the use of "Oga" to address males in positions of power in Yoruba. *Oga* literally means "Big man" (i.e., boss) and it is used across Nigeria, and even in Cameroon, Chad, and Ghana to stroke the egos of men in positions of power and coax them to complete tasks.

I witnessed firsthand how English had been bent and twisted to accommodate different cultural beliefs and experiences in different parts of the world—and not just in places once annexed by the British. This has been an eye-opening experience. So even when we speak one and the same language, the way we do so varies. I learned very quickly that almost every language encodes unique ideas that are culturally unique yet significant, which also explains why much is lost in translation. Familiarizing ourselves with different dialects of English and other languages is, therefore, in our best interest and would make

153

us more effective communicators. In my experience, studying abroad is one of the best ways to acquire a working knowledge of differences in English usage. Videos and media (e.g., YouTube music and movies) from a variety of cultures that we would come across during our travels would also be very beneficial in expanding our language and cross-cultural horizons. Accessing international music and film, for instance, could also make us more approachable and cross-culturally aware.

Most of the countries in which we lived were colonized by the British, so they have continued to use English as their official or quasi-official language. They adopted and adapted English, yielding different brands of English, including Nigerian English, Indian English, and Ghanaian English. These *World Englishes*, as they are termed (see Fig. 1) serve distinct functions that are culturally significant and that are frequently even worded or "sentenced" for lack of a better word (i.e, unique and structured very differently as regards grammar). For example, I recall how my mother was very pleased that she could ask personal questions of the neighbors that came to visit and welcome us when we moved to Igede-Ekiti, a small town in Nigeria. "Are you married?" and "Do you have any children?" she asked. Quite surprisingly, every adult that visited us that afternoon, reported that they had "about four or five children." Even the woman that visited responded using this seemingly ungrammatical sentence. "I have about four children, ma!" she observed in response to my mother's question. I was eight at the time and, while I understood that she used "ma" to mean "Ma'am," I was puzzled by her response. When the men responded in this manner, I assumed that they had very likely lost track of their children, given that polygamy was a common cultural practice, even among those that prided themselves on being "believers." "Yes, I am happily married. I have four wives. I borrowed the best of the old and the new!" retorted one man with a smile that afternoon in response to my mother's query regarding his marital status. When I asked the woman why nobody told us exactly how many children they had, she answered my question with another question. Does your mother count her children?" I had no answer to her question. Noticing my confusion, she attempted to explain using what I now consider a visibly metaphorical and proverbial style of communication. "Exactly!" she continued. "In our culture, we never count our children! Never! Never! Never! Something bad could come to pass!"

Years later, after exploring several African languages, including Swahili, I learned the reason for this seemingly roundabout and 'ungrammatical' way of communicating, once I discovered that Africa has had the highest rate of infant mortality. This phenomenon explains why, to this day, many speakers of African languages avoid mentioning exactly how many children they have.

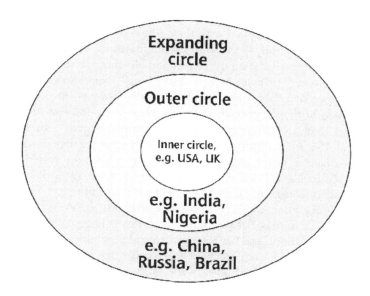

The Four Circles of English (adapted with permission from Braj Kachru who curated the "Three Circles of English" model)

I was initially puzzled when a teacher in Holapur, India (in the state of Uttar Pradesh) asked me for my "good name." "Family name" or "surname' she then clarified. At many birthday parties posted by south Indian families in Nigeria, I returned home with what they called in Indian English a "return gift" (i.e., a gift given to the attendee in return for a gift that they brought).

The most important message we were taught to communicate in every place that we lived in in Africa, as well as in India was respect. Respect was of paramount importance and far more important than any other m else we communicated. overtly encoded/mirrored in both the verbal and the non-verbal language that the locals employed in the different African nations which we had the opportunity to visit, as well as in my parents' home country, India, which I got to visit twice in my childhood: once when I was six and then again four years later. Respectful nonverbal (?) and language were a must, and this meant not looking our elders in the eye, and making every effort to physically lower our posture, gaze and stance in their presence, so that they were always taller than us and got to stand and sit above us literally. When we visited my Uncle in Mumbai and my parents' villages in India, we were expected to bow down and touch the feet of every elder, including our *nani* (mother's mother), *dadi* (father's mother), Uncles, Aunts, and every community member that was our parents' age or older. We also had to address the adults that we met or were introduced to as "Uncle" and "Aunty," even if they were not biologically related to

155

us. Sometimes they would see us coming (ready to bow down) and back away, so that we would be spared contact with their feet and toes, but in all instances, they smiled or laughed joyfully/jovially and in admiration and, placing their right hand on our heads, blessed us with the prayer and blessing "Jeete raho" meaning literally "Keep on living" or live strong and live long!" Sometimes, the women would stick a rupee or other note and *mithai* (Indian sweets) in our hands or pockets as a token of their appreciation for the respect we showed them. They were impressed that my parents had raised us well/properly. In turn, our parents, like the African and Indian parents and elders that we met along the way wanted us to make a good impression, as their reputation rested on our comportment. Showing cultural consonance was therefore essential and what better way to acquire the language of respect and collaboration than in the cornfields outside the classroom? Speaking of cornfields, we even had to go to the school farm twice a week for two hours each time. Digging ridges for yam and cocoa yam, and planting and harvesting corn and vegetables were our weekly "field experiences" and we each received a grade for our efforts in the blazing sun. In my sister's case, she had blisters and gashes to prove that she worked hard. I, on the other hand, would use my communication skills to get the boys to dig up the dirt for me while I excitedly gathered and cracked and munched on oily palm kernels and tomatoes. Can you blame me?

I still remember how the girls in my Form 1B class in southwestern Nigeria sucked their teeth in disbelief and disappointment and rolled their eyes when I called them by their names on the first day that my teacher introduced me to the class. That I had dared to address them by their names when they were visibly older was an error. At first, I could not understand what I had done wrong--to warrant being snubbed and shunned by my Nigerian classmates--when, as a nine-year-old, I unofficially entered Form 1 B, the equivalent of 6th grade in America. Finally, one of the students alerted me to the mistake I had made, albeit indirectly. "I'm not your age-mate!" she insisted when I called her Femi. "Sista Femi is how you should address me!" Better you call her "Aunty Femi" observed a boy named Wole, as he burst out laughing. I couldn't quite understand why he was laughing. "Sista" is fine," Femi retorted, ignoring his laughter and putting him in his place with a look that urged him to show some respect and to mind his own business. His facial expression immediately changed. "I never say you too old!" he responded. "You want respect. She go give you respect!" She scanned his face from top to bottom with a look of disappointment and turned away. "Face forward" she then yelled out to him as she attempted to ignore him by avoiding eye contact. I had learned a valuable lesson in that exchange, namely, that respect for one's elders was expected and part of the communication, even when we communicated using English, the lingua franca of its popular variant, Nigerian pidgin that students and many others preferred to use in informal exchanges with their peers.

Living and studying abroad forces us to pay attention to why individuals communicate the way that they do. In the process, we grow our emotional intelligence, which is arguably more important today than the Intelligence Quotient (IQ). I would therefore encourage you to study and/or travel abroad. You won't regret it and, I guarantee that you won't want to stop exploring.

I learned early on that key criterion for effective communication vary across languages and cultures. Brevity, for instance, is considered curt and rude in the African and Indian settings in which we lived, and even in the U.S., professional communicators are expected to buffer negative news messages. This often yields lengthier messages, yet face-saving goals and fear of litigation frequently supersede conciseness.

Traveling and living outside the U.S. has made me observant, pensive, and, most importantly, inquisitive. My experiences abroad got me to see, hear, feel, smell, taste, and to think in ways I had never thought I could reflect. I haven't stopped doing so since that night when my mother screamed "kabwalala"! I now understand what Frederick Douglas meant when he observed in his narrative that "thinking" got him started and kept nagging at him, catalyzing his initial fear and inertia into self-confidence and action. Listening for and looking for patterns in language behavior, comparing, evaluating, forecasting, and problem-solving have become second nature to me because of studying and living abroad. I've become more observant and detail-oriented and truly enjoy being, first and foremost, an observer.

While we never went on a safari in Africa, animals were not—and are not--walking around freely everywhere, and the savannah doesn't look the same. I can now differentiate between the guinea savannah, the Sudan savannah, and the Sahel savannah. Imagine that! And yes, the first time I saw a giraffe and an elephant was at Disneyworld! As for many other animals that reside in different parts of Africa and India, I got to see them close up at zoos outside their homelands, in America, Canada, New Zealand, and the U.K.

My early and sustained exposure to different cultures, languages, and communication styles has equipped me with a heightened awareness of cultural nuances or subtleties that both signal and explain cultural similarities and differences. In many ways, I am a lifelong nomad, and a part of me still resides in every place in which I once resided. I reflect on my lived experiences and now finally understand that they explain who I am and who I have become, as well as what I yearn for.

Memories of my childhood in different parts of Africa frequently flood my mind, particularly when I feel like I don't belong, as I often do in America. In the silence of privacy-focused America, many a night, my restless mind falls asleep only when it travels through the miles and years to re-hear the *loud* public conversations and the laughter of children playing soccer (called "football" there) with balls made of countless elastic rubber bands strung together, and the chatter of non-stop traffic that speaks volumes through the communicative and protracted honking, and the sounds of roosters' announcing dawn and dusk, and of chickens scurrying and cackling, and goats bleating as they dodge foot and motor traffic, of cows mooing as they swat at flies, and of music blaring in public spaces. Surrounded by this environmental 'noise' for close to 19 years of my life, the silence of public and suburban America is still deafening to my ears. For the longest time, this stark silence kept me awake. The smell of freshly popped corn and fried dodo (ripe plantains) continuously wafts through the miles. Their scent, mixed with the fragrance of frangipani, hibiscus, and marigold, and occasionally too, the cannot-disguise stench of kerosene, petrol, and rot--and the rhythm and dance that is everyday life in those community-celebrative spaces-- call me home.

ANITA PANDEY is a Professor of Linguistics and coordinator of professional communication in the Department of English and Language Arts at Morgan State University, USA. Over the past 22 years, she has taught courses in linguistics, ESL, and business and technical writing. Born and raised in a bilingual home in Africa, she is fluent in French, Hindi/Urdu, Nigerian Pidgin, Yoruba, and Spanish. She earned a BA (Hons.) with a 1st Class distinction in linguistics from Ahmadu Bello University, Zaria (Nigeria), and taught at the College of Education, Azare (Nigeria) before pursuing graduate studies. She received her doctorate in linguistics from the University of Illinois at Urbana-Champaign. Dr. Pandey's research has appeared in *Childhood Education, TESOL Quarterly, Critical Inquiry in Language Studies, Africa Today, Business Communication Quarterly, and Knowledge Management*. She guest edited the millennium issue of *World Englishes* (Blackwell). Her research monograph, *The Child Language Teacher: Intergenerational Language and Literary Enhancement* (Central Institute of Indian Languages), proposes an innovative approach to community language and literacy. She is associate editor of the *Journal of English as an International Language*, guest editor of the 2011 and 2012 issues of the *International Journal of Communication*, and the author of *Language Building Blocks: Essential Linguistics for Early Childhood Educators* (Teachers College Press, 2012). She is also on the advisory boards of four international journals. Email: anita.pandey@morgan.edu

Epilogue

We are inspired by the narratives we shared in this volume. We recognized in the student and faculty/staff stories alike our own experiences as global ambassadors. Morgan State University has plans to expand its campus in Ghana, Asia, and Europe. This will bring more interesting observations from faculty and administrators involved in their creation. Moreover, our university choir travels across the globe and have their own interesting narratives. Our faculty-led exchanges are yet another source of narratives. Finally, each year we welcome a new and robust group of international students to the Bear Cave. We are therefore hoping to capture their and other narratives in a subsequent collection in four years.

Further Readings

We want to share the following bibliographies related to study abroad and international students or minorities students in general for those interested in developing or expanding the programs and resources for their campus community.

Adichie, C. N. (2014). *Americanah.* Anchor Books.

Andrade, L. M., Dittloff, S., & Nath, L. (2019). *A guide to faculty-led study abroad: How to create a transformative experience.* Routledge.

Angelou, M. (1991). *All god's children need travelling shoes.* Vintage Books.

Anya, U. (2016). *Racialized identities in second language learning: Speaking Blackness in Brazil.* Routledge.

Bennett, B. (2020). *The vanishing half.* Riverhead Books.

Bista, K. (ed) (2020). *Global perspectives on international student experiences in higher education.* Routledge.

Bista, K., Allen, R. M., & Chan, R. (eds) (2021). *Impacts of COVID-19 on international students and the future of student mobility.* Routledge.

Bista, K., & Foster, C. (2016). *Campus support services, programs, and policies for international students.* IGI Global Publications.

Bista, K., & Pinder, A. L. (eds.) (2022). *Reimagining internationalization and international initiatives at historically Black colleges and universities.* Palgrave MacMillan.

Blain, K. (2019). *To turn the whole world over: Black women and internationalism.* University of Illinois Press.

Blakely, A., Heywood, L., Stith, C. (Eds.) (2015). *African Americans in U.S. foreign policy: From the era of Frederick Douglass to the age of Obama.* University of Illinois Press.

Coles, R. (1999). *Black writers abroad: A study of Black American writers in Europe and Africa.* Routledge.

El Saadawi, N. (1991). *My travels around the world.* Methuen.

Florvil, T. N. (2020). *Mobilizing Black Germany: Afro-German women and the making of a transnational movement.* University of Illinois Press.

Gaulee, U., Sharma, G. S., & Bista, K. (2020). *Rethinking education across borders: Emerging issues and important insights on globally mobile students.* Springer

Glass, C., & Bista, K. (2022). *Reimagining student mobility in higher education.* Springer.

Glass, C. R., Lin, X., & Bista, K. (2021). *The experiences of international faculty in institutions of higher education.* Routledge

Jarrett, V. (2020). *Finding my voice: When the perfect plan crumbles, the adventure begins.* Penguin Books.

Kincaid, J. (1988). *A small place.* Farrar, Straus, Giroux.

Klassen, T., & Menges, C. (2019). *The essential guide to studying abroad: From success in the classroom to a fulfilling career.* Routledge.

Mbue, I. (2016). *Behold the dreamers.* Random House.

Philllips, C. (1987). *The European tribe.* Farrar, Straus & Giroux.

Sanz, C., & Morales-Front A. (eds) (2018). *The Routledge handbook of study abroad research and practices.* Routledge.Mbue, Imbolo. *Behold the dreamers*

Smith, M. A. (2020). *Senegal abroad: Linguistic borders, racial formations, and diasporic imaginaries.* University of Wisconsin Press.

Stevension, A., & Abraham, K. (2022). *The half yet to be told Study abroad and HBCUs.* The Forum.

Wilkerson, I. (2020). *Caste: The origins of our discontents.* Random House.

About the Editors

KRISHNA BISTA is a Professor of Higher Education in the Department of Advanced Studies, Leadership and Policy at Morgan State University, Maryland (USA). Dr. Bista has published 15 books and more than 75 research articles and book chapters on higher education topics. Previously, Dr. Bista served as the director of Global Education at the University of Louisiana at Monroe, where he was the Chase Endowed Professor of Education in the School of Education. Dr. Bista is the Founding Editor of the Journal of International Students, a quarterly publication on international education. He is also an Executive Vice-President of the STAR Scholars Network, Maryland. He earned his B.A. from Tribhuvan University, M.S. from Troy University, and Ed.D. from Arkansas State University. His recent edited books include *Online Teaching and Learning in Higher Education During COVID-19* (Routledge, 2021); *International Students at US Community Colleges* (Routledge, 2021); *Reimagining Mobility in Higher Education* (Springer, 2022); and *Reimagining Internationalization and Internationalization Initiatives at Historically Black Colleges and Universities* (Palgrave MacMillan, 2022).

ADELE NEWSON-HORST is a Professor of English at Morgan State University, Maryland, USA. She coordinates the Women, Gender, and Sexuality Studies program. She earned the B.A. from Spelman College, the M.A. from Eastern Michigan University, and the Ph.D. from Michigan State University. She has had an illustrious career holding positions in academic administration at Missouri State University, University of Wisconsin-Oshkosh, University of Michigan-Flint, and Florida International University. Her books and articles focus on the literature of African, African American, and Caribbean women writers. She is also the vice-president of the Henrietta Lacks Legacy Group, Maryland. She regularly reviews books for *World Literature Today* and *Academic Choice*. Among other publications, she has published two edited volumes on Egyptian novelist and physician *Nawal el Saadawi: The Essential Nawal El Saadawi: A Reader* (Zed Publishers, 2010) and *The Dramatic Literature of Nawal El Saadawi* (Saqi, 2009).

"This book serves as an important resource for international educators and practitioners at a critical time when institutions are grappling with inequality issues in Study Abroad and student mobility. It offers both practical and research-driven insights that can guide institutional policy and practice in promoting diversity, empathy, and inclusive internationalization on campus."

Ravi Ammigan, Associate Deputy Provost
University of Delaware, USA

"Inequalities in Study Abroad and Student Mobility sheds light on a critically important issue that has been far too often ignored, namely, social inequality in study abroad. Utilizing a comparative cross-national approach, this edited volume offers a highly welcomed examination of a gnawing concern for all of us engaged in international education."

William I. Brustein, Vice President
West Virginia University, USA

"A must-read for all interested in the quality of higher education at an HBCU. Internationalization has long been an integral part of the HBCU history at institutions like Hampton University. This is a timely platform to share the unique ways that the HBCUs have built their institutions on the value of the inclusion of a global population.

JoAnn W. Haysbert, Chancellor and Provost
Hampton University, Virginia, USA

"HBCU students deserve the best opportunities and internationalization of the curriculum and campus is essential to their growth and future opportunities. In Reimagining Internationalization and International Initiatives at Historically Black College and Universities, Bista and Pinder provide a road map for rethinking internationalization at HBCUs and doing it with purpose, a nod to culture, and an innovative spirit."

Marybeth Gasman, Samuel DeWitt Proctor Endowed Chair in Education &
Distinguished Professor, Rutgers University, New Jersey, USA

"This timely book explores the outstanding legacy of global engagement to be found at the nation's historically Black colleges and universities. Higher education leaders at all types of institutions will find the discussion of best practices for internationalization and international initiatives at HBCUs to be both useful and inspiring."

Freeman A. Hrabowski, President
University of Maryland, Baltimore County, USA